FREEING YOUR CREATIVITY

A WRITER'S GUIDE

FREEING YOUR CREATIVITY

A WRITER'S GUIDE

MARSHALL J. COOK

WRITER'S DIGEST BOOKS
Cincinnati, Ohio

Freeing Your Creativity: A Writer's Guide. Copyright © 1992 by Marshall J. Cook. Printed and bound in the United States of America. All rights reserved. No part of this book may be reproduced in any form or by any electronic or mechanical means including information storage and retrieval systems without permission in writing from the publisher, except by a reviewer, who may quote brief passages in a review. Published by Writer's Digest Books, an imprint of F&W Publications, Inc., 1507 Dana Avenue, Cincinnati, Ohio 45207. 1-800-289-0963. First edition. First paperback printing 1995.

99 98 97 96 95   5 4 3 2 1

Library of Congress Cataloging in Publication Data

Cook, Marshall J.
    Freeing your creativity : a writer's guide / Marshall J. Cook.
        p.   cm.
    Includes index.
    ISBN 0-89879-664-4
    1. Authorship. I. Title.
PN151.C64   1991
808'.02 — dc20   91-25535
                                                                                  CIP

Edited by Bill Brohaugh
Designed by Clare Finney

For Ellen

About the Author

Marshall Cook has made his living by writing and teaching writing for his entire adult life. He's examined the creative process — in himself, in other writers, in boat builders and band directors and business leaders — and written about creativity for over 20 years in more than 200 magazine articles and in five workbooks for the University of Wisconsin Outreach.

Cook is a regular contributor to *Writer's Digest* magazine. He also teaches 60 seminars a year on writing and creativity. He lives in Madison, Wisconsin.

Acknowledgments

Thanks doesn't say it, but it's the best I've got.

Thanks to all the good people at Writer's Digest Books. I'd heard horror stories about you big city publishers, but you folks have been so nice to work with. Special thanks to Bill and Catherine Brohaugh, who are wise and nurturing and have helped me so much.

Thanks to my colleagues, to Barry and Chris, Sabra and Ellen, Marian and Beth and the rest, and especially to my mentors, Blake and Arthur. And thank God for a job that allows and encourages me to think new thoughts.

Thanks to my wife's Mom, Dorothy Malloy, whose passion for writing inspires and delights me.

Thanks to my grandfather, William Gilmore Beymer, who recited poetry to me and who let me sit in his den and watch him write.

Thanks to my Mom who, along with all the millions of other things a wonderful mother does for her son, ingrained in me a love of working crossword puzzles.

Thanks to my Father, who taught me discipline and endurance and who gave me my love of baseball and of the outdoors.

Thanks to my son, Jeremiah, who challenges me to be better than I am, for his sake and for my own. And especially thanks to my wife, Ellen, to whom this book is dedicated. She is my soul-mate and master teacher, the one given to me, as I am the one given to her. They give me reason and heart for labor.

Contents

1. What is Creativity?   1

What can we learn by trying to define our creativity? Will caffeine and the Sunday *New York Times* make you more creative? Here, the four myths that limit creative possibilities are busted by the five tentative truths.
Interlude: Creativity Stew.

2. Making Your Writing Your Own   12

Being all of a writer means understanding how the battle between the left brain and the right brain limits creative possibilities. You can rearrange your thinking to win these mind battles and allow your little mind/big mind to team up to enhance creativity.
Interlude: Letting It Happen

3. Writing for Its Own Sake   21

We write because we want to, because we need to, even because we have to. Does your writing end when you finish discovering what you will say, or do you need a reader to validate the process? If you write for fun and for the sake of writing, you're a writer. Journals, letters and low-circulation markets can be the minor leagues that lead to bigger, more lucrative publication.

4. Do You Have What it Takes?   29

Take the "Creativity Quiz" and learn more about your own creativity. Then study "The Creative Personality": Is there really such a thing? And if there is, should you try to conform to the profile?

Introduction

Joy and Rightness

Before I started writing this book, I wrote and self-published a book called *Writing for the Joy of It*. It's a collection of some of my *Writer's Digest* articles and materials I've developed for my writing workshops.

I learned to set type and lay out pages on a Macintosh computer. I found myself becoming mesmerized as the text poured into the forms I had prepared for it, and hours disappeared while I worked.

I also had to learn how to get Library of Congress and ISBN numbers, how to file for copyright and other publishing secrets, all of which seemed scary and mysterious at first and which turned out to be really quite simple and straightforward.

I shopped for a printer and settled on the good folks at Community Printers in nearby McFarland, Wisconsin.

I paid for the books with money I made writing magazine articles and named my "press" after my grandfather, William Gilmore Beymer, a writer and one of my heroes.

I had thought that naming the book would be difficult. (I anticipated so many problems that never occurred.) But the naming came easy. Every time I thought about it, I kept stumbling over the notion of joy. No other word captured the spirit I hoped to put into a book meant to encourage, and maybe even inspire, as well as instruct. And doing the book made me so *joy-filled*. How could I call it anything else?

When those crates of books arrived, they were *totally* mine—in a way unique, I think, to self-publishing.

The job wasn't over, of course. Those books were going to sit there on the floor until and unless I did something to persuade folks to buy them. I wrote news releases, sent out review copies, talked to the buyer at the University Bookstore, prepared a flier, and launched my own modest direct mail campaign. And, of course, I lugged a bag of books with me to workshops and speaking engagements.

I thought I might resent the not-writing parts of the process, but that hasn't been the case at all. Each step has been full of creative challenges and thus full of learning and growth.

I've had lots of reaction, mostly positive, and a few strong reviews. A short write-up in the Sunday *Milwaukee Journal* brought inquiries and orders from area bookstores. But *one* reaction among the many has made me question the title I gave my little book—and prompted me to share this reflection with you.

Rather than assigning a text for my feature writing classes on campus, I ask my students to select one book on writing and write a personal response to it. That way they get to choose something that looks interesting to them, and I get the benefit of many perspectives on many books.

One of my finest writers, Liz Arveson, a veteran reporter returning to school for her degree, chose my book to respond to. What a chance she was taking. What if she hated it?

She didn't hate the book. But she did have a thought-provoking reaction, pointing out the contradiction between the notion of joy I kept stressing, and the grinding "write it anyway" nature of trying to make time for writing and to write creatively on a deadline.

I freely admitted in the book that some of my advice was contradictory. "That doesn't make it any less true," I wrote, "only more confusing."

But my own rather glib explanation doesn't satisfy me now. Here's a fine, seasoned writer telling me that she *hates* to write, just flat out detests the mechanics of putting words to paper.

I mulled and pondered. Okay, I sulked. She had a point. I couldn't reconcile her response with my own feelings about writing, and it wouldn't leave me alone.

An answer emerged in the cadence of an early morning jog. Writing isn't necessarily joyful. But it's *right*.

When I write, I don't always feel elated or even mildly amused. I sometimes experience a hot knot of frustration in my gut. I'm usually fighting the clock. Sometimes words elude me; images slip just out of reach. The beautiful, shimmering vision in my mind taunts me. Nothing I put into words seems half so grand as the idea and the need that compel me to write. Little mind thrashes about, trying to exert control. If it fails, it tightens like a fist.

Joy? Hardly.

But even in the midst of this struggle, someplace beyond or beneath or behind the frustration, I experience a sense of peace founded in the rightness of the task. Not that the words are "right." There's no right or wrong, no template or answer book. There are only these words at this moment. But it's right that I'm writing them. I'm doing what I'm supposed to be doing, what I was made to do.

Only *I* can know this. Only *you* can know if and when it's right for you to be writing.

If it is right, you'll know the feeling I'm trying so inadequately to describe now, a feeling that is much deeper and more secure than mere joy.

I'm being flooded with that feeling as I write these words. I know the words are true for me and that I've written them honestly, from my truth as I'm given to understand it. I know I haven't held back.

In another year, I may be sitting at my kitchen table, writing that "rightness" isn't the right word, isn't really what I meant to say at all, trying again to find words for the rich blessing and the mystery of doing what you're meant to do, which for me means being a writer.

But for now, "rightness" is the word I want.

1

What Is Creativity?

We don't know what, when or how to call it—or even if we should try to call it at all.

It's a vital part of us, that subconscious force that powers our inventiveness, but we're not sure how it works or where it comes from. We marvel at it, rejoice in it, are a little afraid of it when we sense its power at work in us. It feels like the stirring of the spirit or the whispering of the muse.

At the turn of the century, a writer named Charles Haanel called it "a benevolent stranger, working on our behalf."

One writer friend of mine calls hers "Lefty."

Current theory has tracked creativity to the right hemisphere of the brain. But I suspect it will give us the slip again. For all our pondering and theory-making, we still don't seem to understand our creativity very well.

As a writing teacher and consultant, I've coached hundreds of writers over the last twenty-five years, trying to help them get on good terms with their muses. I'm an active freelancer with hundreds of published articles and short stories to my credit, so it's very important to me that I keep in constant touch with my own creativity as well. I've decided that we don't need to label or define our creativity so much as we need to nurture it and learn to accept its gifts. Settling on a precise definition might be a mistake even if we could do it, because in doing so we might limit the possibilities.

This book is all about *not* limiting the possibilities.

Knowing that we won't precisely define or fully understand creativity, let's explore it a bit, beginning with four common myths about creativity.

Myth #1: If I Like It, It Must Be "Creative"

Sometimes when we speak of a piece of writing as being "creative," we really mean that we think it's good or unusual or that we like it. But are "good" and "likable" really synonyms for "creative"? Is a piece of "bad" writing "uncreative"?

The writer goes through the same process, regardless of the outcome. Any piece of writing is the product of the creative process, whether we judge that product to be a triumph or a tragedy. We had better keep evaluations of quality separate from our developing understanding of creativity.

Myth #2: If There's a Lot of It, It Must Be "Creative"

We call people "creative" when they write a lot. Isaac Asimov, Anthony Burgess, James Michener and other prolific producers certainly merit the title. But just as the term "creative" doesn't necessarily apply to the quality of the product, it probably shouldn't apply to the quantity either. James Agee left us very little work, but I'm sure that Agee was exercising his creative powers when he wrote *A Death in the Family*. Harper Lee has published only one novel, but *To Kill a Mockingbird* is as good as they come.

Myth #3: If It Feels Good, It Must Be "Creative"

We also use "creative" to name the feeling we get when ideas and images explode in our minds and the words seem to flow without effort. Musicians talk of being "at one" with the instrument. Gamblers call it "playing a hunch." Athletes refer to this feeling as "the sweet spot" or "the zone." In his book *Healing Journey*, David Smith talks about the sensation achieved while running, a state "beyond meditation" in which the runner seems able to arrive at a subconscious awareness of universal truth.

Everyone from concert pianists to quarterbacks share this experience, and I'm convinced that we can find a "sweet spot" in our writing and tap into our creativity by using techniques we'll explore later. But we need to be careful not to confuse the feeling with the process. Feelings of ecstasy don't define creativity — any more than feelings of frustration and struggle signal its lack. You're creative when the words flow in a burst of euphoria and also when you have to struggle and scratch for every syllable.

Myth #4: If It's Made Up, It Must Be "Creative"

Most of us agree that writing poems, short stories, novels or plays requires creativity. But some might refuse to apply the term to anything that smacks of "journalism," and many folks get downright disrespectful when they talk about writing copy for an annual report or a plumbing fixtures catalog.

In *Practicing History*, Barbara Tuchman complained that nonfiction gets treated like a remainder category. But it's no less creative, she maintained, than other forms of writing. She wanted to create a special name for "writers of reality" and said she would have picked "realtors" if the term hadn't already been taken.

There's no such thing as "noncreative writing." All writing requires creativity, and any type of writing can benefit from a creative approach.

Creativity, then, has more to do with process than with product, more to do with how you approach the task than how well you do it, or how much of it you do, or how you feel about it while you're doing it.

You can bring a creative approach to every step in the writing process — when writing a scene for a novel, certainly, and also when you conduct your library research for that scene and when you later revise what you've written. You're creative when you devise an inventive escape for the hero of your adventure novel, and also when you invent a tasty, nutritious dinner out a refrigerator full of leftovers.

Dispelling these four myths about creativity can help us understand and use our own creativity in our writing. Now, let's replace those myths with five tentative truths about creativity.

Tentative Truth #1: Creativity Is the Triumph of Originality Over Habit

We do a lot of things today the same way we did them yesterday, *because* we did them that way yesterday. As we'll see in chapter five, habit can be as helpful in our writing as it is in other daily endeavors, but habit can also shut out possibilities and cause us to settle for stale ideas and trite language.

For decades, business correspondence began with "Dear Sir." That seemed to work okay until folks began to notice that some of the recipients of that correspondence were she's instead of he's. And some of those she's didn't appreciate being called "sir."

A problem? Sure. "Dear Sir" and the automatic "he" are inaccurate and offensive. But the problem provides an opportunity to be creative, to come up with a new solution.

How many ways can we begin a business letter? Take a piece of scratch paper and a moment (often a powerful combination) and list as many alternative salutations as you can think of. (I'll be asking you to do a lot of scratch-paper thinking throughout this book. You can simply read on if you like, but you'll get more out of our discussions if you dive into them actively.)

Here are a few from my list of possibilities:
• Dear Sir or Madam
• To Whom It May Concern
• Dear Editor (or other appropriate title)
• Gentleperson
• Hi
• Yo!
• Hey You!
• Good Morning

As I look back over the list, some of these possibilities seem downright stuffy. Does anyone really want to be called a "madam"? Others seem overly intimate. What if the person receiving my "Good Morning" missive reads the mail in the afternoon?

Are there other possibilities?

You could call the company and get the person's name. Nobody likes to get "Dear Occupant" or "To Whom It May Concern" mail anyway.

Do we even need a salutation? Many companies have adopted a modified memo form, omitting the salutation and getting right to business.

You might not like any of these solutions, or you might find several to be appropriate, depending on the context. The point is, there are a lot of ways to begin a business letter, most of them better than "Dear Sir," but we never would have discovered any of them if we hadn't confronted a problem that shook us out of the "Dear Sir" habit.

We become more creative precisely at those times of extreme frustration when yesterday's habit solutions don't solve today's writing problems.

Addition to Tentative Truth #1: Creativity Is Often Born in Frustration and Surrender

I often reach a point in my writing where none of my tricks work. I struggle. I rage. Sometimes I give up. And when I give up, my subconscious begins to play with combinations my conscious mind wouldn't dare try. The muse mulls and in its own time proposes new combinations and visions. Sometimes these solutions come in dreams. I've often left a writing problem unresolved at my office, only to have a solution begin to emerge as I biked home. In fact, the basic idea for this book came to me on a bike path on my way to work.

At such times I experience a sudden release of energy and emotion. Most often I'm elated; occasionally I'm filled with doubt. Whatever my feelings, I've learned to accept the gifts of my "benevolent stranger," withholding judgment until later.

Second Addition to Tentative Truth #1: The Farther You Are From a Piece of Paper and a Pencil, the More Likely You Are to Experience a Breakthrough

If you're like me, you don't always get your breakthroughs when you need them. More likely, they come when you're least able to take advantage of them. I do some of my best breakthrough thinking while jogging, bicycling or driving. I think that's because the conscious mind relaxes and lets loose of the problem at such times, giving the subconscious a chance to play.

Can you learn to create these creative moments on demand? Can you schedule your inspirations? Not entirely. Creativity is more like a slot machine than a vending machine. But you can help prepare for and encourage creative breakthroughs, and you can become better able to take advantage of them when they occur. We'll spend the rest of this book exploring ways to nurture and focus our creative power.

Tentative Truth #2: Creativity Involves Making New Combinations

Consider the lowly knock-knock joke. One of our uniquely American forms of humor, the knock-knock joke usually invades the consciousness of fifth-grade boys and takes control for about six weeks. Some kids never recover and are still telling knock-knock jokes at school reunions and business meetings years later.

"Knock-knock."

"Who's there?"

"Sam and Janet."

"Sam and Janet who?"

"Sam and Janet evening, you may meet a stranger . . ."

You get caught leaning the wrong way. If the surprise pleases you, the new combination makes you laugh. If it doesn't please, you groan.

Poetry depends on such surprises based on new combinations of sound and sense. When in the poem "The Miller" Edwin Arlington Robinson tells us that "there are no millers any more," he means both that there's no longer a demand for the trade and that the particular miller we've been reading about in the poem has killed himself. The impact is much greater because Robinson allows us to draw the inference for ourselves. Just as in the knock-knock joke, the poem depends on reader participation and a double meaning for its effect.

You encourage your creativity when you allow yourself to play with new combinations of words, images and ideas—from the silly (knock-knock joke) to the transcendent (poem about the meaning of life).

Tentative Truth #3: Creativity Is the Great Yes

We all learn to say "no" too much and too soon.

"Let me play the devil's advocate," we say when confronted by a new idea, whether our own or someone else's. Then we think up all the reasons why the idea won't/can't/shouldn't work.

Such thinking kills the idea, and it kills all the other ideas that might have come after.

A creative approach means saying yes first. Creativity means playing the "angel's advocate," a term I first heard and embraced when a man named Sydney X. Shore came to my town and gave a workshop on creative problem-solving. Play "What's good about it?" with every new idea, Shore urges. Think of all the reasons why it might work. Let the idea grow. Let is suggest other ideas. Keep open to all the possibilities. Withhold judgment.

When the great animator Chuck Jones, creator of Wile E. Coyote, the Road Runner, Pepe LePew and other cultural icons, called his team together to brainstorm an idea for a cartoon feature, he never allowed negative comments. "If you couldn't say something positive," he says, "you kept quiet." These "yes sessions," as Jones calls them, produced more good ideas than could ever fit into a six-minute cartoon.

Won't you also come up with a lot of silly ideas that way? Sure. The most creative people I've ever met are often fools in the eyes of the world. But what are you really risking? You can always say no later. If you try to choke off the "silly" ideas and only receive the "good" ones, the safe, can't-miss ones, you might not get any ideas at all.

Tentative Truth #4: Creativity Means Getting out of the Way

"The good drawings I do are hardly mine," author and artist Frederick Franck writes. "Only the bad ones are mine for they are the ones where I can't let go and am caught in the ME-cramp."

If you can quiet the yammering of the conscious, controlling ego, you can begin to hear your deeper, truer voice in your writing. Then you'll begin to give yourself surprises of insight and vision. It's still you doing the writing. In fact, it's *more* you. It just isn't the noisy little you that sits out front at the receptionist's desk and tries to take credit for everything that happens in the building.

Tentative Truth #5: Creativity Means Being All of What You Are

Fear makes cowards of us all. We play safe, imitating other writers who are imitating other writers who are imitating other writers. We settle for the trite and true, and when we do, we become less than what we really are.

You must instead become *more* of what you are. Discover your strengths and emphasize them. Become more powerful by becoming more authentically yourself when you write. Only then will you draw fully on the creativity within you and release it in your writing.

What do you have to offer to your reader if not your unique vision, expressed in your unique way? You have yourself to offer, nothing more, nothing less. Offer it all.

When you bring all of yourself to your writing, and when you learn to trust your deepest, most authentic voice and to let it speak in your writing, a creative attitude can pervade and enhance every aspect of the writing process. You experience creatively. You store that experience creatively. You keep open to all the possibilities of expression. You combine images and ideas, eager to see what will happen. You even revise creatively, not sacrificing passion for precision. In this way you fuse intuition and intention.

■ ■ ■ ■ ■ ■ ■ ■ ■ ■ ■ ■ ■ ■ ■ ■
Interlude: Creativity Stew

Yesterday I experienced the joy of a creative explosion. Ideas poured out of me, and I was scribbling notes on envelopes all morning.

Two of the ideas had to do with additions to this book. (As I write this, I have finished the rough draft and intend to let it simmer before tackling the re-creation.) I also had two breakthroughs on a novel I'm writing about a minor league baseball team. All in all, a very exciting morning.

What caused this meteor shower of inspiration? And how can I make it happen again?

I'll try to list all the ingredients in yesterday's creativity stew and see if they add up to a recipe.

• I read one and a half Sunday newspapers. My reading included: Local sports ("Brewers bounce Yankees . . . Packers take a step backwards"); local weather ("Clear, hot and humid"—we got a surprise thunderstorm instead); George Hesselberg's annual summer round-up column; *Parade* magazine's piece on hard-working comedian Jay Leno (moral: if you want success, work for it); Dave Barry as "Mister Language Person"

(I love this guy); a piece on the "World of Poetry" scam (everybody wins a "Golden Poet" certificate and the "right" to buy an expensive anthology); a piece on the effect of steroids on athletes (it isn't good); the latest episode in the adventures of Calvin and Hobbes, in which Calvin and Hobbes play Calvinball, the game with the ever-changing rules. ("This game lends itself to certain abuses," Calvin concludes as Hobbes is about to cream him with a soccer ball.) I also thumbed through the *New York Times* fall fashion supplement, for purely prurient interest. (short skirts are in this season) Did some combination of articles/ideas/images spur my own outpouring?

• While I was reading, I had two large mugs of full-strength, high-octane vanilla almond coffee. Did soaking my brain cells in caffeine stimulate what the think-tankers call "ideation"?

• I ate a grapefruit half and two banana nut muffins. Just the right nutrients for nimble thinking? If I had had Grape Nuts with milk and sliced bananas, would my day have been a creative dud?

• I watched part of CBS's "Sunday Morning" news magazine and caught three segments of special interest to me: a profile of Max Patkin, the "clown prince of baseball"; an obit of one of Washington's finest reporters, Richard L. Strout; and a profile of Dick and Jean Mohanna, who with their son Tim put out the weekly *Cairo* (Nebraska) *Record*. My kind of stories. Did a baseball clown, a Washington reporter and a community editor/publisher team whisper to my muse?

• After breakfast had settled, I went downstairs to ride the exercise bike. I had planned to jog, but the surprise thunderstorm kept me indoors. The brainstorms began occurring while I was on the bike. Did exercise stimulate my subconscious and quiet my yammering inhibitions?

It's getting complicated, isn't it? And there's more, of course, much more. Nothing is simple when we talk about something as rich and deep as our creativity.

• With no alarm to wake us at 5:15, my wife and I slept in until 6:30, when our four-footed alarm, Rosie the Super Schnauzer, decided we'd slept enough. Did all that extra sleep contribute to my burst of inspiration?

• My current bathroom book is Aldo Leopold's *Sand County*

Almanac. I'm marveling at Leopold's insight and sensitivity (he was an ecologist before we had invented the term) and his graceful prose. Did Leopold add to the creative ferment?

• The night before, I watched "Twin Peaks," David Lynch's quirky, moody saga that asks the questions "Who killed Laura Palmer?" and "How many cups of coffee will Special Agent Dale Cooper drink before he figures it out?" I usually don't just watch a television show; I've always got a book, newspaper or magazine with me and split my attention between television (four brain cells), print (10 brain cells) and random fantasy (the remaining 2.8×10^{20} brain cells). But I gave "Twin Peaks" my full attention, and the eerie mood stayed with me all night. Did it also spur my subconscious to yield its treasures?

How far back shall I go?

• I've been writing this book for months, researching it for years, brooding on it for decades. The field was well plowed before the seeds fell.

• I've been a baseball fan since about the time I learned to walk and have haunted minor league ballyards all over the country. The characters from my novel inhabit a niche in my subconscious. Again, it's no surprise that I would receive communication from such old, dear friends.

How much of a part does such life-preparation play in the creative process?

Some of these factors, plus others I've neglected to list, no doubt contributed to my idea-generating morning. I could probably spend the rest of my life trying to figure out exactly how much of which ones were responsible. But that doesn't seem like a very productive way to spend my time. I think it's enough to know that creating ideas involves giving the subconscious plenty to work with and then being receptive when it's ready to surprise and delight.

The caffeine, for example, may help spur idea-generation. Or I may just think it does, which may be just as good. For a lesson on the powerful placebo effect, we turn to the great "Yankee Clipper," Joe DiMaggio, owner of the longest hitting streak in major league baseball history. The great outfielder (you younger readers may know him only as the suave "Mr. Coffee" on television) hit in fifty-six consecutive games in 1941, a record that has been approached (Pete Rose hit in forty-four straight a few years back) but never equaled.

For the first part of the streak, the Great Joe D. used a bat made especially for him. Most major leaguers, then as now, order bats to their exact specifications as to length, weight, taper of the handle and that intangible called "feel" or "heft."

About midway through the streak a fan stole DiMag's special bat between games of a double header. Joe tore up the dugout trying to find his special stick. He went 0 for 3 using another bat, but, with the streak on the line, a teammate persuaded him to use a bat of the same dimensions and similar "heft." Using the counterfeit talisman, DiMag lined a single to left to keep the streak alive.

Did the bat get the hit that kept the streak alive? Certainly not. One of nature's greatest examples of hand-eye coordination did that. But did the bat give DiMaggio the confidence which, blended with his skill, enabled him to keep his streak alive? If he believed that it did, then it did.

Dumbo *could* fly without the magic feather. But he had to take a pretty scary fall to find that out.

Could I re-create my creative Sunday stew by following the same recipe? If I blend two parts caffeine, two parts muffins, a dash of Charles Kuralt, two newspapers and a workout on the exercise bike next Sunday morning, will I come up with another flurry of creative activity?

I might. But I also might sit on that exercise bike until certain parts of my anatomy turn numb without coming up with anything more profound than the observation that I'm sick of pedaling.

There are no guarantees. We can only put good ingredients into the pot, and be ready to taste deeply when the stew is done.

If you're ready, then, let's start cooking your creative stew.

2

Making Your Writing Your Own

Do you want to be a writer just a little bit? Do you want just a little bit to be a writer? I didn't think so.

Don't hold back. Be *all* of a writer. Don't save any for next time. Write it all, every time. There will always be more.

Don't write because you think you should. The world will survive if you never write another word. Don't write simply to practice, getting ready for the "real" writing to come later. Putting in time isn't enough. Put in your life. Risk it all. You'll be tempted to scramble back to safe ground and stale ideas. You must risk losing control in order to become a more happily creative self. You aren't making the writing happen. It's happening in and to you.

Your first commitment is to the writing. Concern for the world's judgment must come later — if at all.

Flannery O'Connor said that when she was writing what would become one of her most famous short stories, she discovered that her main character had a wooden leg. She didn't plan it. She wasn't even conscious of inventing it. It just was. And she knew only a few lines before it happened that the Bible salesman was going to steal that wooden leg. As soon as she knew it, she knew it had to happen that way.

William Faulkner said that he knew his writing was beginning to go well when his characters stood up on the page and cast their own shadows.

This is death to the little mind that wants to control and shape and be in charge. But it's life to the bigger mind, the creative force that allows you to be inventive and original. At such times you're writing for the writing and not for the ego. And at such times, writing isn't just a tool of communication. It's a means of discovery. You can write to find out what you really think and feel.

"I have to write to discover what I am doing," O'Connor says. "I don't know so well what I think until I see what I say."

The poet W.H. Auden once said he liked to hang around words "to see what they would say."

As you grope for the words to express an idea, the idea twists in upon itself or unfolds in new directions and becomes something different. You can write your way into a problem — exploring, defining, clarifying. And you can write your way out of that problem, discovering solutions by giving words to the problems. Through this open, flexible approach to your writing, you learn to tap into your subconscious and focus it on the challenges you face as a writer.

When you see writing as a way of thinking and discovering as well as a means of expressing your thoughts and feelings for others to share, writing becomes an indispensable part of your life, less destination than journey, less something you do than something you are.

"When I was young I thought that we climbed a mountain to reach a plateau," poet Donald Hall writes. "Now I know that we climb to climb. . . . The work is the thing and not the response to the work."

You write, then, not fundamentally for whatever fame and fortune it might bring to you, but for what the process does for you. And as you become concerned about the quality of the writing, you worry first not for the sake of the reader or the market, not for the sake of your own ego, but for the sake of the writing itself. What does the writing need in order to be complete and truthful? What must you remove that is less than the truth and thus unworthy of the writing?

When you write for the writing, you are enriched by the process, regardless of any other outcomes.

"No writing is a waste of time," writer Brenda Ueland assures us. "With every sentence you write, you have learned something. It has done you good. It has stretched your understanding. I know that. Even if I knew for certain that I would never have anything published again, and would never make another cent from it, I would still keep on writing."

The ultimate goal of the writing, Ueland maintains, is nothing less than "the enlargement of the soul" of the writer.

Put another way, writing expands your creative powers at the same time that it draws upon them.

Approach each writing encounter as if it were your first. Let yourself feel the anticipation that is part fear, part exhilaration, part expectation that something wonderful will be created in you.

Don't try to reproduce yesterday's vision. Seek today's new vision.

Your writing affirms your life. Writing about the details of your life says that those details matter. Even the writing you do from out of your frustration, depression and despair indicates that these feelings are important and, thus, that your life matters. Writing is an embrace of life, with all its sorrows and contradictions, and an affirmation of the creative power within you.

My cat Tuffy used to revel in a spot of sun, rolling and stretching and sticking her paws in the air. She didn't wonder how the wonderful warmth got there. (At least I don't think she did.) She didn't judge it or evaluate it or compare it to yesterday's sun spot. She just rolled and stretched and slept in it. Writing can be like that, a reveling in the wonder of whatever it is you're writing about.

Writing is openness to the universe. It is deep stillness, a listening.

The Battle of the Hemispheres: Left Brain Versus Right Brain

Writing creatively, which is to say writing with that deeper, truer voice within you, involves a partnership between two somewhat diverse sets of skills and impulses. First you generate ideas and images. (Or sometimes, on those most exciting but perhaps as yet rare occasions, you feel driven by ideas and images demanding that you express them.) Then you struggle to express those ideas and create those images clearly, for their own sake and perhaps for the sake of a reader.

We have made the process into somewhat of a war between "left brain" and "right brain." The "creative" right brain generates ideas spontaneously, like a reckless child, the theory goes. The killjoy left brain then restores order, perhaps even scolding the child for its sloppiness, and tries to mold and shape the creation into something presentable.

We characterize the two hemispheres as sort of an Oscar/Felix odd couple. Left-brain Felix keeps his half of the operation tidy. He craves order, loves lists, has a lot of rules about what can and can't, should and shouldn't be done. He trusts reason over intuition. He's goal-oriented. He'll work hard to please.

Right-brain Oscar stays out all night, eats cold pizza for breakfast and sleeps until dusk. He's driven by whim and intuition, which makes him erratic but also makes him incorruptible. You can't threaten or bribe him; he creates strictly for the joy of it.

Felix works to make sense; Oscar plays to have fun.

This way of defining two contradictory facets of our nature isn't really new. We've called them by many names, going back to the ancient Greeks and their head/heart split. Freud wrote of Id and Ego. Contemporary therapists speak of parent and child. On those terms, creativity is our child at play; evaluation is our adult at work.

The metaphors work as long as the partnership runs smoothly. But what if a dispute erupts? What happens, for example, if your free-spirited child gets tired of seeing its ideas rejected or altered beyond recognition? Your prodigy might just stop producing those ideas at all—a suffocating state we call writer's block.

Even when not locked in internal warfare, many writers demonstrate an imbalance between the two sides of their creative natures. Some are dynamos at generating ideas but have an awful time expressing them clearly. They fill journals and notebooks with titles for stories, names for characters, first lines for poems, fragments of a work ever in progress but never progressing beyond the idea stage. We might say of such folks (who are you and me at one time or another) that the right side of the brain is dominating.

Others like to research and revise but dread the confrontation with the blank page or screen. Has the left brain become so dominant that the creative side has withered and withdrawn?

We try to solve such problems by learning to keep the partners in their proper places in the creative process. First let your child play freely. Withhold judgment while you explore possibilities and approaches. Then bring the adult in to reject and refine. If you begin to judge too soon, you'll surely turn off the flow of ideas.

Good advice, as far as it goes. But even when you withhold judgment until the proper time, you still may encounter problems if you see the process as a battle between opposing forces. Haven't you played a rather cruel trick on your muse if you let it create freely but then change everything it has created? "You can have your fun," you seem to be saying, "but all that play is really silly and wasteful. I'll take over now and do the *real* writing."

You might just revise the passion right out of the writing. And your muse, spurned by your rejection, might stop generating those "silly," "wasteful" ideas that are the basis for everything you create.

You must never belittle your "dumb" ideas.

It works the other way around, too. Later steps in the process should be no less creative than the initial inspiration. Don't get grim when it's time to rewrite and edit. At every step you must use your creative power, must bring your excitement, energy and openness to your work. In refining your original vision so that others can share it, you must not rob it of its urgency and its truth. Stay open to joyful inspiration.

Little Mind/Big Mind

Rather than worrying about left brain/right brain, it might be useful for you to think in terms of "big mind" and "little mind." Little mind is that conscious, rational part of you that plans your day's schedule, outlines your writing project and worries about making the mortgage and car payments on time. But it is only a small part of that bigger mind that is constantly at work, waking and sleeping, remembering and dreaming, feeling and reacting. Writer Natalie Goldberg calls that larger part "Wild Mind" because the thoughts, images and impulses it produces are sometimes disorderly and disrupting. Little mind spends a great deal of energy trying to suppress these kinds of thoughts, because they are threatening to the order little mind has worked so hard to make from the chaos of the world.

But if you write only from little mind, ignoring the contributions from big mind, you will create little thoughts—ones you have seen elsewhere and which seem safe.

There must be no war—not between left brain/right brain or between little mind/big mind, id and ego, child and adult. Creativity has a single source. You must use all of you when you write. Your writing must be passionate and precise, must express your intuition and your intention.

■ ■

Interlude: Letting It Happen—
What Teaching Taught Me About Writing

On the first day of what has thus far been a twenty-five-year teaching career, I stood before my 8:00 a.m. freshman composition class, set my typewritten notes on the podium and began to read. I don't think I looked up once. I was afraid to.

I didn't know any better. I had been lectured at. Now I was doing the lecturing.

I didn't ask for questions. I didn't want questions. I had every word scripted. A question might have spun the class right out of my control and into chaos. I didn't know, then, how wonderful a little chaos can be.

Poor students! Their first college class, and some skinny geek not much older than themselves reads to them for fifty minutes. They probably didn't know any better either, which explains why nobody took an ax to me to stop the endless droning.

I kept up this note-reading for several weeks. Researching and writing all those words was awfully hard work, especially when coupled with the enormous task of "fixing" their weekly writing assignments. But I figured that's what a teacher did, so I shouldered my burden willingly.

That most subversive force in the world, the human smile, began to erode the wall I had erected at the front of the classroom. I glanced up from my notes occasionally and caught a student actually paying attention, if not to my words, at least to me. Students greeted me outside of class. (How strange "Professor Cook" or even "Mr. Cook" sounded.) It gradually dawned on me that these folks were human beings.

Then one late fall morning, mid-drone through my 8:00 a.m. comp class, a feeling somehow managed to bubble up through my protective wall of words and pop into my consciousness. The feeling resembled the one I used to get as a child about two weeks into summer vacation. I was bored. I was boring myself. And I was getting to do all the talking! What must the poor students be feeling? (Or perhaps they were beyond feeling.)

I made it through the lecture, but I was shaken. From that

day, I began, quite tentatively at first, to let go of my absolute control of the classroom. I began — horrors — to let my students talk.

I found many eager to share their thoughts. But, to my dismay, I found that most were afraid to speak up. "Class participation" was just another teacher trick, a club used to force compliance, a grade in the ledger. Discussion was a game of trying to guess what the teacher wanted to hear.

So I began to develop ways to coax out some real talk, some truth. We sat in circles. I refused to talk. I used guerrilla theater tactics. My colleagues and I spent endless evenings swapping stories from the trenches. This was late in the '60s, remember. We thought we were freeing the slaves.

Gradually, a few students began to trust, and I began to relax and to mean what I said when I told them to say what they meant. I set the agenda, yes. I offered guidelines. I kept the discussion on track. And I still held the gradebook, whether I wanted the power of intimidation or not. No matter whether we sat in circles, or I stood up in front of the class while they sat in rows, we were still penned in a gray box with chalkboards.

But classes were no longer scripted, no longer so strictly under my control. Students digressed, told their stories, tried out their ideas. They surprised me and each other. We laughed together. The English language survived. Their compositions got more honest. The more honest they got, the fewer grammar problems I had to "fix."

I kept struggling to find ways to help them take responsibility for their learning. We did a lot of talking about their writing. They did most of the talking. Their insights startled me. They were able to say almost all the things I would have said about their work. And they came up with insights that never would have occurred to me.

They were no longer just writing for an audience of one, the professor, a captive audience at that. They were writing for each other. It made a big difference.

About the time I figured I knew it all about the discovery method of teaching writing, I learned something new and wonderful from newspaper editor Clarke Stallworth of the Birmingham, Alabama, *News*.

"I used to take a reporter's copy and fix it," he said in his rich Alabama drawl. "Hell, I knew what was wrong with it. So I'd make it right and give it back to them. And they hated me for it."

This sounded a lot like the teacher/student relationship. Why the animosity? Weren't we just trying to help?

"I was taking their stuff away from them," Stallworth explained. "It wasn't theirs anymore. It was mine."

You have to keep the copy in the reporter's hands, Stallworth said. Talk to them about their writing. Ask questions. Then shut up and listen.

"They know what's wrong with it," he said. "Let them fix it."

It's the process, not the product, that matters most here, Stallworth said. Fix it, and you get one piece of good copy (maybe). Let the reporter fix it, and you get a better writer.

"I thought it was the copy," Stallworth said. "But that ain't it. It's the growth of the reporter."

How much more so for a student. I'd been "fixing" their writing for twenty years, taking it away from them and making it mine — even making it sound as if I'd written it. After talking with Stallworth, I tried a new method. Now I don't make a mark on their work. Instead I write a critique — sometimes rather lengthy, reacting first as a reader, not a teacher, pointing out strengths as well as weaknesses, asking questions, making suggestions, proposing alternative approaches and, sure, pointing out the misspelled words and the dangling modifiers. Then we talk.

This way takes a lot longer. It's a lot more work. It requires more thought. It's worth it.

I've lost a lot of control. I've gained a lot of new possibilities, a lot of excitement in the classroom, the thrill of knowing that I don't know exactly what's going to happen. The give-and-take can be quite exhilarating on a good day, almost always surprising on any day.

My learning has been gradual, an evolution rather than a revolution. But when I compare my teaching now with that of that scared lecturer at Santa Clara University twenty-five years ago, I know I've come a long way.

As with the teaching of writing, so with the writing itself. I am still learning to let go of some of my control and to let my writing surprise me. I try to write, not just from my narrow, controlling little mind but from the wider, freer big mind. Little mind is so careful, so timid. Little mind allows no laughter, no tears. But big mind lets it all tumble out, opens up to all the possibilities, tries things out just for the adventure of seeing what will happen.

The key is to use it all, at all points in the writing process — when you conceive of ideas, when you research them, when you discover your themes and your truth as the words begin to emerge on paper or screen, as you review and revise those words later, as you search for kindred spirits to publish your words.

It's the work of a lifetime.

3

Writing for Its Own Sake

I've been getting ready to write this book for a long time.

I've been trying to put stories on paper since I could hold a pencil, and I've been teaching writing for twenty-five years. I've learned from instruction, from experience, from confronting questions I couldn't answer, from talking with other writers, from giving and getting criticism.

I've interviewed scores of creative people — writers and editors, boat designers and inventors, entrepreneurs, and hydroplane jockeys. I've been storing up stories, opinions and ideas about creativity and how it works in the writing process for a long time. Being a writer, I naturally wanted to write it all down.

After I sent my proposal for this book to Writer's Digest Books, I got busy on other projects and tried not to think about the discussions that might be taking place in Cincinnati, Ohio. But as I was walking across campus one early spring morning, I caught myself thinking, "I sure hope they let me write this book." (How could I be human and *not* think such thoughts? Don't you think them, too?) But then I had another thought, one so empowering it left me joy-filled and energized. "Of course you'll write this book," said a friendly voice inside my head. "That's *your* decision to make."

Others can judge your work. They can decide whether or not to publish it. But only you can decide if, when and what you'll write.

You write, first and fundamentally, for the writing itself. All else is secondary. When you allow yourself to approach writing in this way, you liberate your sense of possibility, the basis of your creativity. Write authentically, what you want and need to write, and you will write creatively:

- because you'll be expressing your vision, in your way,
- because you'll be more willing to take the risks that lead to discovery,
- and because you'll be willing to work much harder, with more concentration, energy and sense of purpose, when you write from your own motives.

Not all writers write for publication and the money and recognition it might bring. Not all writing has a large audience — or any audience at all. We write because we want to, because we need to, even because we have to. We write for what the process of writing can do for and to us. For some of us, writing is as much a part of life — and as necessary — as breathing.

Writing for Yourself

If a tree falls in the forest with no one there to hear it, does it make a sound?

Of course it does, some say. The same cracking and rending and snapping takes place, with or without a listener. And yet, others would argue, the transmission of sound isn't completed until the sound waves wiggle the little bones in somebody's inner ear. So in a sense there really isn't any sound until someone receives it.

It doesn't really matter, a third would say. The tree's on the ground, whether anyone heard it fall or not.

Does your writing end when you finish discovering what you will say, or do you need a reader to validate the process? Is reading enough, or must the reader make sense of your words? Must that sense be the meaning you intended, or is it okay for the reader to draw her own conclusions? How much and what kind of reaction is enough in order for the writing to matter?

I've kept a journal since my son was born. I don't write in it every day. In fact, sometimes weeks go by without an entry. But if I'm not working on anything else, and sometimes when I am, I'll often make a journal entry at some point during the day, usually first thing in the morning. I tend to write a lot when I travel, and especially when I'm alone, so my journal has become a part of all my journeys.

I don't intend for anyone to ever read my journals. So why do I write them?

First of all, I read them—usually not right away, sometimes not for years, but eventually. When I do, I encounter a different self, a fellow who sometimes amazes and often embarrasses me. I see how much I've changed and how much I've stayed the same. I see recurring themes in my life and in my writing about my life. I note progress so gradual I wasn't aware of it in the day-to-day living of it. I understand my journey better.

The journal entry I made this morning is an act of faith and hope, a gift I trust some future self will be there to receive.

Sometimes I glean material for stories and articles from my journal. I use the journal to store observations, first lines, story titles, descriptions and scraps of dialogue, and I hope they'll ripen before I come back for them.

For example, I made a journal entry after taking my young son Jeremy to the local gym to watch his dad participate in a city-league basketball game. Months later, I discovered the entry, and discovered, too, that my subconscious had apparently been mulling the incident, giving it shape and meaning.

I wrote a short story called "Parting Shot" based on this journal entry. The story was published in a literary magazine and anthologized in a collection of fiction. I'm still proud to read the story to my classes. The protagonist isn't me, and the boy isn't my son, but the characters and the plot grew from that journal entry.

Much of what I write in the journal has no such useful function, however, and often the seeds I plant sprout weeds or fail to sprout at all. But I write anyway, not just to store images and ideas for possible later use, but for all I gain through the process of creating them in words. My journal is like a gymnasium for my creativity, and I emerge from each workout strengthened and invigorated.

When I try to put my life into words, I give it new shape and meaning and find out what I'm really thinking. Words collide. One word suggests another. I escape to a tangent that is better than the road I had intended to take and which leads me to my deeper, truer self. My mind begins to relax. The chattering receptionist at the front desk takes a break, and a quieter, wiser voice emerges.

This isn't always fun. I keep that babble on in my mind to drown out difficult realities. But opening myself up to those realities, exploring them, allowing myself to react honestly to them, never seems to hurt me. Freud called the subconscious a "beast in the basement," but I don't think it's a beast at all. It's a child, a friend, a lover. It's my truest, best self, the one who has been with me since birth. It's all the doubts and fears and joys and hopes my little mind isn't big enough to grasp and make sense of. To touch this chaos is, I think, to touch the universal.

I suppose you could call this exploration a kind of therapy. But there doesn't have to be a problem, and I don't expect to be "cured." The exploration is never-ending.

I write; therefore, I am. I write; therefore, the one who is writing has some value, some purpose and meaning. Sometimes my journal entry makes an otherwise frustrating, unproductive day feel like a success.

By keeping a journal, I become more alert, more open to the life around me. I might try to write about this later, my subconscious seems to say, so I'd better pay attention to it now. I want to get it right, which is to say not that I will make any brilliant observation or draw any profound conclusion but simply that I will record the life around me carefully, accurately, respectfully.

This kind of heightened awareness makes life more exciting. Nothing is mundane when I really pay attention to it. And I'd better pay attention, because I can't write it if I never saw it in the first place.

I have vivid memories of the minor league ballparks I've enjoyed a ballgame in, the side roads and the countryside I've explored, the diners I've sipped coffee in, the sunrises I've witnessed while jogging on unfamiliar trails. I experienced them intensely, in part because I knew I'd want to write about them in my journal.

The same kind of heightened attention can enrich the everyday and the familiar—my bedroom with dawn flooding the windows, the tilt of my dog's head when I talk to her, the lake path shrouded in morning fog.

Such specific images can give life to my writing. When I reach for these images now, they appear for me, not because I am gifted at invention or recall, but because I paid attention.

In that way, attention fuels creativity. It's such an important part of the creative process, in fact, that we'll spend the next chapter exploring it in detail.

I have one more reason for writing in my journal—it delights my heart. I know that's not true for everybody or even for most folks.

But I'm a writer, and I love to write, love to feel the pen in my fingers and to see the words form on the page, love to empty my true self into the writing, love to struggle to get it right, love to see how it comes out.

Kids skip rope and climb trees for animal joy. Adults set up elaborate model train layouts in the basement, train bonsai trees, work on their golf games, just for fun. Can't we write for fun, too? For a long time I didn't think so. I thought writing only "mattered" if someone published it and paid me for it. Thus, I was constantly concerned with the "acceptability" and "relevance" of everything I wrote. Ironically, such thinking limited my ability to create the kind of original, authentic writing that stands a much better chance of being published. When I began to lift my restrictions, writing more freely and more creatively, I began to publish more, too.

If you write for fun and for the sake of the writing, then you're a writer. You didn't need permission, and you don't need to publish, to be a writer. And you mustn't ever let anybody tell you different.

Writing for an Audience of One

When my family left California to move to Wisconsin in 1979, I left behind some good friends. One fellow in particular left a big hole in my heart. I worked alongside my friend Boomer Clark, battled the administration with him, lifted weights, shot hoops, drank beer and traded stories with him. We were close.

He didn't answer my letters, and yet, when I went back for a visit, we picked up our friendship right where we'd put it down. He hadn't forgotten me. He just doesn't write letters.

It seems that most folks don't these days. Letter writing is a dying craft. But maybe because I think with my fingers, and maybe because I've never felt comfortable with a telephone, I still write a lot of letters, including an occasional letter to my friend Boomer.

That's writing for an audience of one. It feels like a conversation. I can see and hear the recipient as I write. My writing takes on the same tone I'd be using if we were talking face to face. I review the events of my life as I think about what sorts of things my friend would be interested in hearing about.

"Good practice," I tell myself, to justify spending the time. Writing letters probably does do me some good as a writer, in the same way that journal-keeping strengthens the writing muscles and keeps the creativity limber. But I think letter-writing is worth doing for its own sake, and I hope the recipients of my letters think so, too.

I've had another, more involved experience with writing for an audience of one. I started keeping my journal about the time my son, Jeremy, was born, not with any thought of documenting his growing up but simply because I was so full of emotion, I needed someplace to put some of it.

For his eighteenth birthday, I decided to give him a gift of time and labor, a gift of self. I began combing almost eighteen years' worth of journals, looking for descriptions of his activities, observations about his growing up, a bit of the social context of his life. I planned to weave them into a slender volume, but *The Life and Times of Jeremy Cook* swelled into a sizable manuscript. I learned and felt an awful lot in the process.

I had Jeremy's book professionally bound and presented it to him on his birthday. He didn't say much at the time. I suppose he would have preferred a sports car. But he took the book with him when he went to college, and he has told me that he has read it often and that it means a lot to him to have it.

I don't believe anything I've ever written has given me more satisfaction.

Writing for a Small Audience

Would you write your family history, in the hope that it would entertain, enrich and inform your grandchildren some day? It would be a gamble, wouldn't it? Who's to say they'll be interested in grandpa's or grandma's ramblings? But if you don't write that family history, who will? Is it worth the risk?

Who will chronicle your organization's growth and development? Who will dig out those vital stories about your town and put them into article or book form?

Nobody who's looking for a mass market, because that market just won't be there.

Is the writing any less valid or important because it serves an audience of ten instead of ten thousand? Are you any less of a writer for having served that "lesser" audience? Will you learn and grow any less while writing for that audience?

Recently my side road ramblings led me to discover a tiny Wisconsin town named Cooksville. The town seemed to consist of perhaps eight or ten or a dozen houses, a church and "The Cooksville General Store." I was captivated, both by the store and its name, and so I stopped. Along with the usual crackers and cereal, chewing tobacco and kitty litter, the store offered a pamphlet for sale up by the cash register that purported to tell the history of the town. I bought a copy and read about the town's founder, John Cook—no relation, I'm fairly certain—and the development of the town.

The pamphlet's author won't make the best-seller list with this work. I doubt if there was much profit in it at all. But I'm surely grateful for all the work that went into it, for I learned a great deal and had my curiosity satisfied.

Publishing such a pamphlet, or having a short story published in a literary journal with a circulation of two hundred, might lead to bigger, more lucrative publication. The small presses can be a proving grounds, a minor leagues of sorts. And the audience, though small, may be influential. Publication of one of my stories in a literary magazine led an agent to call me and, ultimately, to represent me in what turned out to be a futile attempt to get a novel published.

But if you never progressed beyond those low-circulation markets, would you consider yourself a failure? You'll have to answer that question for yourself. You must assess your motives and evaluate your goals as a writer. If you find that nothing short of a best-seller will satisfy you, then by all means figure out what it takes to achieve that goal and devote yourself to it.

But no matter what you hope to achieve as a writer, from the personal growth and heightened awareness of journal-keeping to books in the windows at B. Dalton and a guest shot on the Carson show, you need no outside validation or verification to call yourself a writer. If you write, you're a writer.

And whatever your goals, you'd better love the process of writing. You're spending a lot of your time, a lot of yourself, on it. That's the only certainty.

Some tribes of American Indians use long distance running as a form of worship. As they run, they sometimes chant a kind of mantra that translates roughly: "I was born running. I will always be running. I will die running." In that way, they don't become anxious about the destination. They give themselves totally to the experience of running, living completely in the present moment.

Could you feel that way about your writing? No matter what the goal, allow yourself to become absorbed in the journey. You may or may not get to the top of the particular mountain you've chosen to climb. Reconcile yourself to the trail. Enjoy the scenery. Learn the rhythms of the hike. Become the climb.

Other rewards may come in due season. When they do, you may be too absorbed in your writing to notice.

4

Do You Have
What It Takes?

Do you consider yourself to be a creative person? Or have you decided that creativity is only for the chosen few and that you just
don't have "it," whatever "it" is?

Here's a brief "creativity quiz" to help you decide. This is not a
scientifically devised test, and I offer it in a spirit of fun. But your
answers may help you to understand and appreciate your creativity.

With that in mind, sharpen your pencils, put your books on the
floor, keep your eyes off your neighbor's paper, and let's begin.

■ ■ ■ ■ ■ ■ ■ ■ ■ ■
Creativity Quiz

Pick the response that best completes each statement for you.

   1. Most of my dreams tend to resemble:
      a. my waking life.
      b. episodes of "Twin Peaks."
      c. a foreign film without subtitles.
      d. I don't dream.

   2. My earliest memory most closely resembles:
      a. stealing a kiss behind the pergola in first grade.
      b. eating my first solid food — a spoonful of strained beets.
      c. getting slapped on the behind by a guy wearing a mask.
      d. I'm pretty sure I had a sausage pizza for dinner last
      night.

   3. When faced with a problem I can't immediately solve, I

tend to:

a. ignore it and hope it goes away.

b. scream and curse—and then ignore it and hope it goes away.

c. tackle it with a smile, trying to think of as many solutions as possible.

d. I subscribe to the old adage, "If at first you don't succeed, give up."

4. My desk looks like:

a. a hospital operating room before an operation.

b. a hospital operating room during an operation.

c. a hospital operating room after a tornado.

d. I don't have a desk.

5. The sight of the setting sun makes me want to:

a. fall asleep.

b. sing an old love song.

c. compose a new love song.

d. Who looks at sunsets?

6. When I'm not around, my friends describe me as:

a. "old reliable."

b. "a little zoned out."

c. "from another planet."

d. How do I know what they say when I'm not around?

7. When I was in grade school, teachers wrote notes on my report cards that said:

a. "not working up to potential."

b. "relates well with the other children."

c. "destined for greatness."

d. I burned my report cards years ago.

8. I have to be in the mood in order to:

a. write.

b. write well.

c. feel good about what I wrote.

d. I'm never in the mood.

9. The hardest part about writing is:
   a. getting started.
   b. finding the time.
   c. knowing when to quit.
   d. hauling all of those publisher's checks down to the bank.

10. I would characterize myself as:
    a. a little bit creative.
    b. pretty creative.
    c. a supernova of creativity.
    d. about as creative as zucchini.

Give yourself five points for every 'c' response, three for each 'b,' zero for an 'a' and minus five for a 'd' and find your score on the following scale:

45-50: Shove off, Shakespeare. We're talking creative genius here.

40-44: What are you reading this for? You should be writing your own book on creativity.

35-39: You're at least as good as the guy who writes the gardening column for the local paper.

30-34: You should be able to work up a shopping list without too much trouble.

25-29: You *are* about as creative as zucchini.

Below 25: Have you checked for a pulse recently?

As you've probably guessed, the scoring is all in fun. I don't think any test can tell you whether or not you're creative. But let's see what this silly test *can* tell you about your creativity.

1. Most of my dreams tend to resemble . . .
2. My earliest memory most closely resembles . . .

The key here isn't so much *what* you dream or remember but *that* you dream and remember. Dreaming and remembering are remarkably creative acts. We combine ideas, images and sense impressions to make new ideas and images. We may even receive inspiration or answers to problems in our dreams. We all do it, although some tend not to remember their dreams.

Have you ever had a dream you couldn't understand? Or one that you thought naughty? How can that be? How can *you* have a dream that *you* don't understand or approve of? Are there two you's?

Left brain/right brain theory explains it this way. When you sleep, left brain lets go of the controls, freeing right brain to make its crazy movies without subtitles. Anything goes. There are no rules or taboos. When you remember the dream with your waking, rational mind, you may be confused or shocked.

If you think in terms of little mind and big mind, imagine your dreams occurring in big mind, that vast expanse of sense impression and intuition that accepts no rules or limitations. The confusion comes when little mind tries to apply its standards of logic and literal meaning to dreams not governed by any such rules.

Memory is as creative as dreaming. We used to think remembering involved storing static bits of data marked "Family picnic, July, 1957" and the like and then calling up the intact memory, like looking at old pictures in a photo album. Except that sometimes the memories come into consciousness unbidden, and sometimes they evade your best attempts to retrieve them.

It isn't such a neat process of filing and recalling static experiences at all. Turns out, you store impressions in bits and pieces, recombine those bits and pieces and then remember what you created. Your version of "Family picnic, July, 1957" will be like nobody else's remembrance, in part because your experience was different at the time, but also in part because your recollection is an act of creative storytelling.

3. When faced with a problem . . .

However you approach your problems, I suspect that you become your most creative when yesterday's solutions don't work on today's dilemma. You must learn to embrace these apparent blocks as opportunities to create something new and wonderful, a solution that not only works but that surprises and delights. The ability to apply creative methods to problem solving in writing isn't a gift, reserved for the few. You can do it, and you can learn to develop your ability more fully. We'll explore specific methods for dealing with your creative opportunities in chapter twelve and the Miracle Writing Plan at the end of the book.

4. My desk looks like . . .

I'd love to believe that messiness is a sign of creativity. If you'd ever seen my desk, you'd know why I feel that way. Fact is, my messiness indicates that I'm messy and nothing more. It's not what is or isn't on your desk but what's going on in your mind and your receptivity to your own creative bursts that really matter.

5. The sign of the setting sun makes me . . .
6. When I'm not around, my friends describe me as . . .

We're dealing with stereotypes here. You may or may not be moved by a sunset, and you may or may not be a wild and crazy party person. Such traits don't have a lot to do with your ability to write with originality and flair. Creativity is as likely to show up dressed in a three-piece suit as in jeans and a T-shirt, as likely to be found sitting in a corporate boardroom as hunched in front of an easel.

7. When I was in grade school . . .

I know a lot of very creative people who got great grades in school, who exhibited marvelous social adjustment, who were active in extra-curricular activities and won citizenship awards and perfect attendance medals. And I know a lot of very creative people who got held back in or kicked out of school and whose idea of an extra-curricular activity was smoking in the lavatory.

Academic achievement and social adjustment don't seem to serve as good indicators of creativity one way or the other.

8. I have to be in the mood in order to . . .

We're treading hard on another stereotype here, the picture of the suffering writer, waiting days, weeks, months for inspiration while drinking heavily and looking tragic.

Erase the picture of the garret. Replace it with an image of the newsroom in a modern daily newspaper an hour or so before deadline. One reporter sits steel-rod straight, tie tightly knotted at the throat, buttons buttoned, nails trimmed, hands on the keyboard, eyes on the screen. A second paces and mutters to herself as she composes her lead in her head. A third sits with untied sneakers planted firmly on the desk, keyboard in lap, back to computer screen, chair tipped back within an eighth of an inch of crash landing.

The neat ones and the sloppy ones, the male ones and the female ones, the thick ones and the thin ones, all have one thing in common. They're all writing. Not a case of writer's block in the bunch. How come? Because they can't afford to get writer's block. They just write. And because they've been at it awhile and learned their craft, the stuff comes out pretty good, whether they're "in the mood" or not.

Yeah, but that's just journalism, you say. But journalism is no less creative than poetry. Different aims, different forms, sure. But there's no such thing as "uncreative writing." If a reporter can create on deadline, whether "in the mood" or not, you can write your way through the down times, too.

9. The hardest part about writing is . . .

Why should there be a hard part at all? If you were really creative, wouldn't the words just roll out of you? If you have to struggle, doesn't that indicate that you're not really creative?

I used to think so. Then I read Carlos Baker's marvelous biography of Ernest Hemingway and came to understand how hard Hemingway worked, how much he revised, "to get the words right." I read Joseph Blottner's biography of William Faulkner and realized that writing for Faulkner was often about as easy as pulling your own impacted wisdom teeth. I read the collected works of sportswriter Red Smith and learned that for Smith writing was a simple matter of sitting down at the typewriter and opening a vein.

At first my disillusionment made me discouraged. If it was such hard work for Hemingway and Faulkner and Smith and other great writers, how could I hope to write well? But then I began to look at it another way. Precisely because it was so hard for Hemingway, and because writing is as much craft as art, perspiration as inspiration, there's hope for us, too. By working hard, you can learn to write well and to make the most of your creativity when you write. Whatever part of the task is hardest for you, you can focus your creative energy on it and learn to do it better.

10. I would characterize myself as . . .

You're not just creative. You're wildly creative. You exhibit your creativity every day, in dozens of ways that are so graceful, so much a part of your natural response to the world, you're not even aware of them. You use your creativity every time you dream, every time you remember, every time you solve a problem, every time you make a joke or plan a menu.

How do you *know* you're creative? Same way you know you're in love. You just do. You can't prove it, but you can see the results.

If your writing doesn't make you feel at least a little bit hot — angry, excited, giggly, desperate — then you might not yet be writing out of who you really are. You might be writing somebody else's vision, using somebody else's words. That doesn't mean you're not creative. It means you haven't yet freed your creativity.

If you're starting to feel get-naked-and-roll-in-a-snowbank excited when you write, you're on the right track.

But even if you feel rotten when you write, that doesn't mean you're not exercising your creativity. And it doesn't mean the writing isn't any good. Your emotion is a reaction to the process, not the product, to the act of writing rather than to the quality of the writing itself.

The Creative Personality

Some folks have isolated certain clusters of traits that comprise what they call the "creative personality." According to psychologist Abraham Maslow and others, these traits include:
- high amounts of energy, enthusiasm and a general zest for living,
- a well-developed sense of humor and the ability to laugh at yourself,
- a high level of tolerance for uncertainty and ambiguity,
- a problem or project-orientation,
- a need for and ability to make productive use of solitude,
- independent thinking and a tendency to question conventional wisdom,
- openness to new ideas.

Other characteristics of the creative personality, according to the experts, include playfulness, willingness to risk failure and to be different, the ability to withhold judgment and a general openness to the environment.

Creative people seem to need to be creative, even when it's impractical or costly to do so. Creativity seems to be a source of joy, of relief from boredom, of solace from pain, and of just plain animal fun.

Most of the terms we've used so far to describe creative people indicate our respect, admiration and even envy for those we consider to be creative. But there is a down side. "Childlike" can also be "childish" in the creative personality. Independence and a need for solitude can translate into rudeness and a stubborn streak. A tolerance for ambiguity can also mean a tolerance for heaps of debris on the floor and old pizza crusts in the underwear drawer.

And many studies have found a high correlation between creativity and mental illness and a high incidence of suicide, alcoholism and depression among creative people. One source says that 80 percent of creative people suffer from some sort of mood disorder. Recent studies debunk this apparent connection, so we need to be pretty careful about taking any of this too seriously.

So what does it all mean to you and your quest to make richer use of your creativity in your writing? Is there really a creative personality? If so, should you try to conform to the profile?

Trying to Find Woody Allen Funny

Let's suppose that, while you were reading that list of characteristics of the creative personality, you cringed a bit when you got to the part about "a well-developed sense of humor." Maybe you consider yourself to be a relatively humorless person. While others are roaring at the office wag's latest joke, you find yourself wishing you were someplace else. Woody Allen movies have never provoked even a giggle, and you tend to skip the comic page.

If you feel that this dour assessment fits you, first let me congratulate you on your self-awareness and honesty. Accuse most folks of almost anything else, and they'll let it slide. But tell someone he doesn't have a sense of humor, and you might just have a fight on your hands.

But if Maslow and others say you should have a sense of humor in order to be creative, then maybe you'd better start trying to find the humor in a Woody Allen flick.

If you do, I think you'll be making a mistake on two counts.

First, violating your deepest sense of yourself is probably as uncreative an act as you could ever perform. Your sense of what is and isn't funny is a natural, integral part of who and what you are. You can't change it, and you shouldn't try.

And second, Maslow and his fellow analysts are writing descriptions, not prescriptions. They are describing characteristics they have observed in a great many — although certainly not all — people they otherwise judge to be creative, and then coming up with a composite they call the "creative personality."

That's a great deal different than trying to develop a recipe for creativity: take two parts sense of humor, add a dash of solitude and two tsps. schizophrenia.

It just doesn't work that way.

So what can we learn from personality profiles? To find our answer, let's look for the common thread that binds all of these creative traits together. Can you find a word or phrase that would describe the kind of person this list would represent? Take a moment and jot down any words that come to mind. In your list, you'll find your answer.

The word I keep coming up with is "openness."

A creative attitude seems to involve:

- an *openness* to experience,
- an *openness* to possibilities,
- an *open mind* about ways to go about solving a problem,
- and most of all, instead of walls closing us off, an *open door* to pass through in discovering new abilities, new interests, new powers.

Can you learn to become more open? Can you catch yourself closing up when you should be opening, shutting down when you should be turning on, quitting when you should be getting ready to go another round, putting yourself down when you should be giving yourself a chance?

Yes, you can. I've written this book primarily to help you do just that.

We're all part rational Felix, part intuitive Oscar. And we're all creative in our own ways. You should certainly try to remain open to new ideas and to withhold judgment until you've explored all the possibilities. But your creativity must flow naturally out of who you are. If you feel the urgent need to make sure all of your forks are lined up properly in the silverware drawer before you sit down to write, then do it, regardless of where that seems to place you on anybody's creativity profile.

To paraphrase the song, you must do it your way.

Now let's look at a few barriers that may be stopping you from doing just that.

5

What's Getting
in Your Way?

If you're so endlessly creative, how come the writing isn't going so well—or at all? How come it's so hard to get started? How come a process that should be so joyful feels so painful sometimes? How come you can handle a hundred creative challenges a day without faltering, but the blank computer screen can stare you down?

Chances are you're getting in the way of your creativity.

That receptionist out at the front desk has gotten so good at screening out the unwanted messages, it's screening out the ones you want and need, too.

You create the block. You can take it down again.

How Fear of Flopping—Or Flying—Keeps Us Cooped Up

When I conduct workshops on creativity, I often ask my guests to list any fears they have concerning their writing. Their answers are often revealing. Take a few moments, if you'd like, to make your own list.

Are you afraid of rejection and ridicule? Most of us are. What if you attempt a writing project and find that you can't pull it off? What if you write from your heart, and your reader doesn't respond? What if you work for weeks on a piece, polish it carefully, mail it to an editor—and get the dread rejection slip?

You hurt. You hurt a lot. And all these things will happen. If you try, you will fail—many more times than once.

You must confront your fear of failure, recognize it as a normal part of the process, and then work despite your fear. Risk all, one word at a time. Write first for the sake of the writing, for the ideas you must express and the stories you must tell. If you're committed to the writing, and if you believe in what you've written, you'll be able to handle the world's rejection.

But will you be able to handle its acceptance?

Did you include "success" on your list of fears? What if someone actually publishes your stuff? Will they expect you to do it again — even better next time? What if your words really move people? Are you ready to accept that responsibility?

What if you become the star of your autograph party at the bookstore, the darling of local talk radio? Will you have to buy a new hat to accommodate your swelling skull? Will you get so carried away with Being a Writer, you won't have time, energy or inclination left for writing?

Not if you keep coming back to your fundamental motivation. You write first for the writing. If you struggle always to strike out any word that is false, your standards will enable you to endure even something as potentially corrupting as the world's adulation.

You're the same person, and your writing is the same writing, whether it's rejected by the local shopper or lands atop the *New York Times* best-seller list.

Don't let fear of failure or of success keep you from becoming the writer you can become, regardless of the world's opinion.

Squelchers May Be Cramping Your Creativity

What's the worst thing anybody has ever said to you about your writing? Spend a few moments with this, and, if you want to, write those negative comments down.

Early in my journey as a writer, I had a short story returned with an obscene rejection letter. No simple "doesn't meet our editorial needs at this time" from this fellow. My little story was an affront to his existence. He told me, in terms I wouldn't use here or anywhere else, to stop wasting my postage and his time.

I was stunned. I felt as if I'd been kicked. How could my little story have engendered such disgust?

I read the story over. I had loved it when I sent it off to this vile man, and I loved it as I reread it. Sorrow and humiliation turned to anger. What was the matter with this lunatic? Even if the story were bad (and I clung to the belief that it *couldn't* be *that* bad), the response seemed so out of proportion, like killing a gnat with a howitzer.

I put a patch on my bleeding ego, gathered my courage and sent my story off to another potential assassin—who promptly accepted it. And when my story appeared in print, I saw to my soul's delight that the magazine also carried a story by the miscreant who had tried to kill me with his criticism. He had to have seen my story nestled right up next to his. Sweet revenge!

But what if I had never sent that story out again? What if I had believed that editor's awful judgment and quit writing? I would have denied myself one of the deepest pleasures of my life and been cut off from a source of great satisfaction, personal development and monetary reward.

We must never give that kind of power to uncaring strangers.

Not all squelchers are vicious. Some aim to teach you—as when an English teacher circles your misspellings and writes "deadwood," "awkward" and "unclear" in the margins. Friends and relatives may try to protect or guide you. ("Yeah, but what will you do to earn a living?")

Some of the people you show your work to just won't care much about it. Perhaps that's the worst put-down of all.

But no matter the source or the motivation, squelchers can rob you of much of your creative power by diminishing your willingness to take risks in your writing. If you approach the blank page fearfully, you may write to avoid errors rather than to create work that has power and integrity. You may try to sound like somebody else whose work seems to be accepted. In doing so, you become considerably less than yourself. Better to be boring than to be a fool, you may think. Better a yawn than a guffaw.

Not so. Risk the guffaw. Anything's better than a yawn. There's nothing cautious about creativity. It dives and darts against the flow of traffic, risking all for the sake of getting where it knows it must be. And then, safe on the other side of the stream of traffic, it may gather itself, flash a quick grin at the oncoming drivers, and race back again, having determined that the other side wasn't where it needed to be after all.

Have you absorbed some squelchers into your soul? If so, you must exorcise them, for the sake of your creativity. Chant those squelchers until they begin to sound as silly as they really are. Exaggerate them until they pop like over-inflated balloons. Talk about them with a fellow writer or a friend. Shine the light on these demons of the darkness, and they will disappear.

But it isn't always that easy. If you're not careful, the poison of negativity can seep into your subconscious and shackle your creativity from within your own mind. If you have internalized any hurtful put-downs (and we all do to some extent), you must catch yourself having the negative thoughts and then talk back to them.

It has taken me years to catch all the squelchers rumbling around in my subconscious and to learn to talk back to them. The process continues. It's worth the continuous effort, because it frees up energy and will for creative effort.

Here are a few of the squelchers that plagued me, along with some of the positive talk-back I learned to replace them with.

■ ■

Squelcher	**Talk-back**
You should be doing something worthwhile with your time.	You're assuming that writing is a waste of time. That just isn't so.
You should be doing something worthwhile with your time.	Says who? I have a right to relax.
You should be doing something worthwhile with your time. (This business of "wasting time" was a big issue with me.)	Other peoples' writing has enriched and illuminated my life. Perhaps my writing will, even in a small way, do that for someone else. What could be a better use of my time?
Nobody's going to take your writing seriously.	Says who? My observations are as "serious" as anybody's.
Nobody's going to take your writing seriously.	So what? The only judgment that really counts is mine.
Nobody's going to take your writing seriously.	Sure they will. They have before, and they will again.

Who told you you could write?	Who told me I couldn't?
Who told you you could write?	Who needs to tell me?
Who told you you could write?	I told me!

The longer you write, and the more success you enjoy with your writing, the easier it becomes to create — and believe in — your positive "talk-back" statements.

Take a moment now to isolate just one of the squelchers you may be carrying around inside you. Write it down. Just giving it shape and substance on paper will begin to lessen its power over you. Now begin the process of destroying that power completely by writing as many "talk-back" statements as you can think of.

Do this with as many squelchers as you can think of. Whenever you catch yourself in the grip of one of these put-downs, review your list of talk-back statements and add to them.

Does this sound like brainwashing? It isn't. You've *been* brainwashed. Or perhaps "braincluttered" is a better term. Now it's time to begin ridding yourself of the junk you've let others store in your head.

Meanwhile, keep away from those who have a negative word to say about everything. If you can't yet tell yourself what you must hear — that you are a writer the moment you start writing — find someone who *will* tell you.

Some Rules About Rules

"There are three rules about writing a novel," Somerset Maugham once said. "Unfortunately, nobody knows what they are."

Rules govern how you assemble words on paper. These rules create a web of common assumptions between writer and reader, so that your reader can understand and trust you. You misplace a modifier or misspell a word at the risk of destroying that understanding and trust. You must master the basic rules of grammar and usage, just as a carpenter must learn to handle hammer and nails, plumb line and level.

But writing is much more than rules. Writing is communicating ideas and emotions. Writing is changing your reader's life. You must do whatever it takes to make the writing work, and that means you must be willing to question the rules.

Who said you must never end a sentence with a preposition? Why did they say it? Does it make sense? (Or will it produce a nightmare such as "That's the kind of nonsense up with which I will not put"?)

My teachers taught me never to begin a sentence with "and" or "but." But I do it all the time. I'm not intentionally defying Mr. Wilson, the cynical taskmaster who forced me and my classmates to work on grammar sheets for a full semester in eleventh grade when we were supposed to be studying American lit. And (there it is again) Mr. Wilson wasn't lying to me when he taught me that rule. He was teaching me term-paper English, 1961 style. This isn't 1961, I'm not writing term papers, and beginning a sentence with a coordinate conjunction has become standard practice.

You must go beyond the rules when it will help your writing. Will you dare to boldly split an infinitive if the resulting phrase sounds better to you? Will you knowingly commit a sentence fragment in order to emphasize your point? Possibly. If used purposefully. And not overdone.

The Non-rule About Rules

If you've got a reason to break a rule, do it. Otherwise, follow the standard rules of grammar and usage (as best outlined in the grammar book for adults, *The Elements of Style*, by William Strunk and E.B. White). We'll talk more about grammar in chapter fourteen when we take up the topic of revision.

If your subjects and verbs tend to fly in opposite directions, don't decide that you'll never be a writer. Learn the rules as best you can. Write your vision. Share your stories and your insights. Revise carefully. Then do it again. If the writing's still a mess, hire somebody to edit it for you.

Healthy and Unhealthy Habits

My big brother Dale taught me how to drive in his (later my) 1951 Chevy. He drove us up into the San Gabriel Mountains just north of Altadena, California, my hometown, parked the car on what seemed to me to be about an eighty-five-degree angle, slid out from under the wheel and challenged me to try to get the car into first gear.

It seemed impossible. First I'd keep the clutch in too long, racing the engine frantically while we rolled down the hill. Then I'd pop the clutch out too fast, sending the car lurching forward until the engine died with a scared gasp.

For days I couldn't get that car into first. Then one day I could. We actually moved forward. It was a revelation, one of the great moments of my life. I did it again. And then again. The more times I successfully feathered the clutch and eased the car into gear, the easier it got. Soon it became so easy, I didn't have to concentrate on it so hard, and I could actually look out the windshield and see where we were headed.

I've driven stick-shift cars ever since. Other than a brief orientation to each new car I pilot, I never have to think about the once formidable task of feathering the clutch and shifting gears. It's as if my hands and feet have learned how to do it, and my brain doesn't have to worry about it anymore.

Same thing goes for learning how to construct a sentence on paper. Making sure that each sentence has at least one subject and one verb and that the verb is on proper speaking terms with its subject has become "second nature to me now," as Rex Harrison sang in *My Fair Lady*, "like breathing out and breathing in."

Grammar becomes a healthy habit. The longer you write, the more healthy habits you develop. Once the basics of writing become second nature, you're free to concentrate on other, more subtle writing decisions, such as mood, tone and point of view. You can look out the windshield and see where you're taking your passenger, the reader.

But habit can become unhealthy when you automatically apply old, learned responses to new creative challenges. You want to describe the torrential downpour hammering your hero. You reach into the semantic grab bag and come up with "raining cats and dogs." The phrase leaps to mind because you've heard it so many times. But that's precisely why you have to reject it and dig deeper. Your reader has heard it many times, too, and so it has lost its power to move her or to evoke an image. She won't hear the screeching or feel the sting.

In fact, *you* won't hear or feel anything when you write such a tired phrase. That's one way to tell for sure that you're dealing with a habit response, a trite solution to a problem demanding freshness. No feeling in the writer, no feeling in the reader.

You must reject the first "right answer" and search for a better one. Leave the phrase and keep going, but know that you're going to come back to it later. When you do, close your eyes and try to experience the kind of rain you're attempting to describe. Write as many words or phrases as you can that describe that rain. Select one that works and that is consistent with the tone you've established. If no winner emerges, simply write "It was raining hard" and go on. They aren't all going to be gems, and a plain statement is better than a fancy cliché.

Excuses, Excuses . . .

We sometimes have good reasons not to write. If the invitations have been sent out, the minister, priest or rabbi arranged for and the hall rented, you'd better go ahead and get married and work on the novel another time.

But when do reasons become excuses?

Take a moment to complete these "after" and "if only" statements. Don't stop with one ending. Write as many as apply to you.

"I'll get serious about my writing after . . ."

"I'd write more and better if only . . ."

Here are a few "after" and "if only" statements. Do any of them look familiar?

I'd write more and better if only I had . . .
• gone to college,
• taken a creative writing course,
• gone to a writers conference.

I'll get serious about my writing after . . .
• things settle down a bit in my personal life,
• the kids go to school,
• I retire.

Reasons—or excuses? Let's find out. Take each of your "after" and "if only" statements, read them aloud and then ask yourself, "Why wait?"

Who says you have to take a creative writing course before you can start writing? Write now. If you find a course or workshop that will help you do your work better, by all means take it. But meanwhile you can be teaching yourself how to write, can be exploring some of the ideas and stories inside you, can be discovering yourself as a writer. Why wait?

Perhaps you're worried about not being good enough to start. That's like sitting on the edge of the pool, refusing to join your swimming instructor in the water because you're not a very good swimmer. You may not want to jump in the deep end quite yet, but you'd better get your bathing suit wet if you ever want to improve your skills.

You may be suffering from the "Shakespeare Syndrome." The shadow of the Bard of Avon (or some other much-admired writer) may be shielding you from the light of your creative sun. "I'll never write that well," you lament, "so why try to write at all?"

The world doesn't need another Shakespeare. It doesn't need another Elmore Leonard or Louis L'Amour, Joyce Carol Oates or Bobbie Ann Mason. The world doesn't need another anybody. We've still got the work of the originals. We need you, writing with your authentic voice and out of your unique vision. You don't have to measure your writing against Shakespeare's yardstick or anybody else's.

Did any of your "after" and "if only" statements survive the "why wait" test? If so, read them aloud and this time ask, "When will that be?"

If I waited for conditions to become perfect for writing, I'd never write. How about you? It's hard to make time for writing when the demands of job and family can be so time-consuming. But if you really want to write, you'll make that time, starting now, not in a vague future that never comes.

Of course your family, friends and colleagues need you. But you have the right and the need to devote a part of yourself to your writing. And when you do, you'll be a better helper for those who depend on you.

If statements remain on your list, they may in fact be valid reasons for you to postpone making your commitment to writing. Perhaps you lack some of the fundamentals of composition, for example, and sense that trying to write now would be like trying to type while wearing boxing gloves.

Do whatever you need to do to get those boxing gloves off. But that doesn't mean you can't write in the meantime. Keep a journal and write in it every day. While you're getting ready to become a writer in one sense, in another sense you're already a writer — and through the practice and discipline of regular writing, you'll be getting better and better at it.

Shed the excuses. Deal with the reasons. Get on with the writing.

Making Time to Be Creative

Carol wakes up at 5:15 a.m. to the news on the clock radio. She quickly showers and dresses and makes breakfast for husband Del and the twins, Alex and Andy — eggs over, soft but not runny, a once-a-week treat for Del, who's watching his cholesterol; raisin bran muffins and fruit salad for the twins. She deftly bags the kids' non-identical lunches, being careful to leave the butter and mayonnaise off Alex's baloney and cheese sandwich and sprinkling grated carrot on Andy's.

She barely has time for her raspberry yogurt and a quick scan of the newspaper. She does a few stretching and breathing exercises while she goes over her notes one more time for the presentation she must make later that morning.

On the way to work, she decides to forgo her daily session with her cassette tape series on time management so that she can visualize her presentation going exactly as she wants it to go.

So it goes, another hectic start to another hectic day in the life of an American superwoman — successful businesswoman, mother and wife. The presentation goes well, as do several meetings with clients. She picks up the groceries and drops off the dry cleaning on the way home from work and has homemade vegetable soup on the stove and biscuits in the oven by the time Del gets home from work. (They split the cooking and shopping duties, and it's her week.)

And when it's all over — with the kids tucked in, the business reading done and tomorrow prepared for — Carol finally has a few moments for herself. She sits down at the family word processor, calls up the short-story file, rereads the several attempts she has made at a beginning, stares at the screen for several long minutes, and then turns off the computer in frustration edged with rage.

She's just too tired to write, and she can't concentrate because she's already under the pressures of tomorrow's killer schedule.

Carol obviously has a flair for coping that borders on creative genius. She's a doer who pushes aside barriers and uses her creative problem-solving abilities to juggle the challenges of family, career and personal needs.

But for all her creativity and productivity, she's having trouble finding time — and energy — for her secret ambition — to write and publish a short story.

She never will find it. And neither will you.

You aren't going to find the time to write. Nobody's going to give it to you. You have to *make* the time. And you must give your writing prime time, not leftovers.

Since nobody has yet figured out a way to add a twenty-fifth hour to the day or an eighth day to the week, you'll have to make time out of the available materials. Approach this problem as another creative challenge.

So often when I'm confronted by such a challenge, I respond with a list of all the reasons why I can't. Do you find yourself reacting this way?

"I'm already exhausted."

"I can't find the time for a lot of things I want to do now — like reading the complete works of Mark Twain or going to the ballgame."

"I can't take time away from my family."

"I don't think my boss would like it much if I told her I didn't get the report done because I was writing my novel."

If you react this way, you're responding with what Sydney Shore calls "the automatic 'no.' " Instead, begin with the assumption that you *will* make time each day for writing. The question becomes "how," not "if."

Start by examining the way you spend your time now. You could even keep a log for a week or so. Jot down what you're doing every fifteen minutes. At the end of the week, comb through the log, looking for activities you could eliminate or trim. You may find that, with just a bit of shifting and tucking, you're able to free up fifteen minutes, half an hour, maybe an hour a day you didn't know you had.

In my daily schedule, I found two areas where I could easily extract almost a full hour of writing time. First, I realized that I didn't need to watch both the 6:00 and 10:00 local news. (The world would probably keep on spinning if I skipped both, but I *like* news.) Second, I curbed my raging crossword puzzle habit, cutting down from three a day to two and sometimes even one (the thought of going cold-turkey gives me the sweats). And I put a time limit on each puzzle — which actually turns out to make the game much more fun.

I'm not advocating that you try to jam every second with productive activity. Time spent with feet up and mind untethered lets the creative well refill and refreshes the soul. You may need to take a walk on a clear, crisp surprise of a spring day and to spend a rainy Sunday afternoon looking through the old photo albums. Parents need to spend goof-off time with the kids. I need to walk the dog at least as much as she needs to be walked.

I'm also not advocating that you build a shelf for your typewriter in the shower stall or strap a notepad to your steering wheel. Shower when you shower, drive when you drive, and write when you write. But you could paste the pages of your short story to the window over the sink and revise while washing dishes, if that's the only way to get the work done. Writing and driving don't mix, but you might talk plot ideas into a tape recorder on the way to work.

What are you willing to give up to gain precious writing time? Ernest Gaines gave up his lunch hour, eating quickly so that he could spend his time writing on the paper sack his lunch had occupied. He wrote that way for years, until the "overnight" success of *The Autobiography of Miss Jane Pittman* freed him to write full time. Elmore Leonard got up at 5:00 a.m. to do his writing before going to work at an advertising agency. He wrote five books and thirty short stories that way before big success with novels such as *Glitz*, *Killshot* and *Bandits* freed him from the day job.

But it didn't free him from hard work. He still writes from 9:30 a.m. to 6:00 p.m., five days a week, and "some on most weekends," he says.

If a careful combing of a typical week's activities doesn't yield the time you need for writing, make a list of all the ways you could create that time. Note everything you can think of, from large, radical life changes to smaller, less drastic modifications. Take a few moments to make your list now. Don't reject any ideas. Just let them come.

My list included major changes (quit the job, divorce the spouse, auction off the kid . . .), medium-sized alterations (sell the house and buy a maintenance-free condo) and small tinkerings (get up thirty minutes earlier, combine two coffee breaks into a writing break . . .).

Set your list aside. Come back to it in a couple of days and circle the ideas that seem reasonable. Make a commitment to try out just one of those ideas. You'll be fighting strong habit patterns, so you must keep at your new routine for at least three weeks before deciding whether or not the change is successful. Resist the impulse to say, "I can't do it." You created your old pattern; you can create a new one.

At the end of three weeks, evaluate your new life. Are the disruptions worth the gains? Look for ways to minimize the stress your writing may put on the rest of your life. If things just aren't working out, go back to your list and pick out another possibility for a three-week trial run.

"I Got Rhythm, I Got Rhythm . . ."

As you make a place for writing time in your daily schedule, take into account your biological highs and lows, so that you can write when you're most energetic. Most folks have two peaks and two valleys every day. I'm a morning person. I become fully awake before dawn and charge into the day's activities. I feel creative, vibrant, fully alive in the early hours, peaking around noon before sliding into my post-lunch stupor. I start to get charged up again in late afternoon, and my steam carries me until about 10:00 p.m.

I do my writing during my morning peak time, when I'm eager to find out what I'll say. I research or revise during the afternoon doldrums. I often read in the evening.

Whenever you schedule your writing time, treat your appointment with computer, typewriter or pad of paper as seriously as you would an audience with the Pope or a meeting with the President. You may be nervous about your "date" with your muse. You may dread what has in the past been a snarling confrontation or a bitter standoff. After we examine start-up techniques later on, you may find yourself looking forward to your writing sessions. But no matter how you feel about the appointment, keep it. Don't allow yourself to think, "Oh, well. It's only writing. I can always do it tomorrow." Would you say, "It's only eating. It's only sleeping. I can always do it tomorrow"? If you're a writer, writing is as essential to your well-being as eating and sleeping.

When you say, "I can always do it tomorrow," perhaps you're really telling yourself that your writing isn't important (and, by extension, that you're not very important either). If so, you've unmasked the statement for what it really is, a false and destructive squelcher. Talk back to it! That kind of message would kill you if it could.

■ ■

Squelcher	Talk-back
My writing isn't important.	Say's who? If I say it's important, then it's important.
My writing isn't important.	My writing is an affirmation of my life.
My writing isn't important.	My writing is as important as anybody else's.

Since your writing *is* important, don't be bashful about establishing your writing time. Tell your family and friends about your new schedule. Make it stick. Writing time must be inviolate. If you believe this, others will believe it, too.

A guest at one of my writing workshops had been making great progress on a novel, but an invitation to a dinner party threatened to wipe out her scheduled writing time — and the marvelous momentum she felt her project taking on. So she stole away from the after-dinner conversation, brought her pad and pencil into a shower stall and wrote for almost an hour before she was discovered. She was definitely serious about keeping that writing appointment!

Family and friends don't cause all the interruptions. Sometimes the enemy is within. Do you catch yourself hoping the telephone will ring? Get an answering machine, turn it on and resist the urge to answer. Do you invent dozens of little errands — to the pencil sharpener in the den, to the telephone directory in the kitchen, to the stationery store for a new ribbon? Get all your materials assembled in your writing place, so that you can use your writing time for writing.

A Place of One's Own

Your writing place doesn't have to be fancy. You don't need a book-lined den with a picture window. But you do need a place that's just for writing, so that you don't have to pitch your tent and dig your trenches every time you want to make camp. If you can leave all your materials where they fall at the end of a session, you'll eliminate a lot of start-up and break-down time. That rules out the dining room table, but that old desk behind the furnace in the basement would be perfect. We'll talk a bit more about establishing a special place just for writing in chapter ten.

The "Do It Anyway" Principle

Okay. You've cleared the time and the space. You've kept your writing appointment. And you don't feel like writing. You feel like doing anything but writing. You even feel like mopping the kitchen floor or giving the family Newfoundland a bath instead of writing. What do you do?

You write anyway.

Remember, you don't have to be in the mood to write—or to write well. Your writing will be just as good as the stuff that flowed out of you when you were euphoric. It will take longer, and you'll feel awful. You'll suffer, but the writing won't.

Create deadlines and quotas, and then work to fulfill them. Be realistic, so that you can be firm. "I'll write the first three chapters of my novel by Friday" probably isn't realistic, especially if you've never written any chapters before. To set such a deadline is to set yourself up for failure and a powerful reason to quit trying.

Is five pages a day a reasonable quota? Is one? You must decide. Set a goal that makes you stretch but not snap.

Perhaps you'll work better with a time-and-effort goal rather than a production goal. "I'll work hard for three hours" may be an effective goal for you.

Can you create on demand? Yes, you can. We'll talk about preparation and process in later chapters. For now, be assured that productive writers develop schedules and stick to them. Humor writer Dave Barry says if he waited to be inspired, he'd write about two columns a year. When Barry and other professional writers don't feel like writing, they adhere to the "do it anyway" principle. People who can't afford to have writer's block don't get it. That tells you everything you need to know about writer's block.

It helps to have more than one project going. You might be temporarily stuck on one piece but ready to work on another. Work far enough ahead of deadline so that you can set a project aside for a bit and come back to it with enough time to meet your own or an editor's expectations.

But if the deadline is approaching and the work must be done, hunker down and do it. If you apply your skill, your energy and a creative attitude, the work will be fine. The reader will never know how you felt while you were writing.

Does all this hunkering down mean you can never take a vacation, never slough off for a day or even a couple of hours? I don't think it means that at all. From the spontaneous picnic on a sunny spring day to the well-planned three-week trip to Ireland, vacations fill the well, help us to see the world from new angles, refresh and energize us.

But you might find that you can never really get away from the writing. For some of us, writing isn't a job or a hobby. It isn't something we start and stop. It's a natural part of who and what we are, something that goes on, consciously and unconsciously, all the time.

Scheduling and discipline are necessary, but keep open to inconvenient inspiration. Be on call twenty-four hours a day, notepad on the night table, journal in the pocket or purse, mind alert and receptive to the stirrings and promptings of the subconscious, that mysterious friend who offers you wonderful gifts if you will only be wise and humble enough to accept them.

6

The Art of
Paying Attention

In Captain Augustus McCrae, novelist Larry McMurtry created one of his most memorable characters.

McMurtry has written many powerful novels, including *Terms of Endearment, Last Picture Show, Buffalo Girls* and *Horsemen Pass By* (made into the movie *Hud*). But *Lonesome Dove* is my favorite. In this sprawling saga, ex-Texas Ranger McCrae turns rustler and heads out on a cattle drive that symbolizes the dying of the old ways and the Old West.

Out of the whole long, wonderful journey, I remember most vividly one small bit of advice from McCrae: "The only healthy way to live is to learn to love all the little everyday things."

That's the only way to write, too.

Teachers and writing guides constantly advise us to "Show, don't tell." Good writing thrives on detail. We must render a scene vividly in order to convince a reader of its reality and to enable that reader to experience it with us. As Brenda Ueland says, "The more you wish to describe a Universal, the more minutely and truthfully you must describe a Particular."

When you struggle to describe a forest path, to create a bit of dialogue between lovers, to reproduce a smile or frown or shrug or snarl, you constantly call on the details you have stored and re-shaped in your memory. But you can't write about things you haven't really seen or heard, tasted or touched. We learn early to squeeze the awesome torrent of sense impression into a manageable trickle, to take in only what we need in order to go about our business. We do much looking, Frederick Franck says, but little seeing. "We know the labels on all the bottles but never taste the wine."

An Encounter on State Street

I see him from half a block away. And I know he sees me.

He's a short, scruffy man in clothes a short step up from rags. His eyes flick over me and dart away. His right hand extends an inch or two toward me, palm up—not enough to violate the city ordinance against panhandling, but enough to make it clear he wants me to give him money.

Now that I've noticed him, I have to deal with him—ignore or acknowledge him, give him money or walk by. I have to feel guilty or outraged, sad or superior—or something.

It would have been so much easier not to see him at all.

I spend a lot of energy screening out such sights—anything distracting, offensive or just simply irrelevant to the course I've set for myself. Surely such screening is necessary. But it's also destructive for a writer.

Imagine—as Ralph Waldo Emerson once did—that you could see the stars for only one night in your life. Wouldn't you stay up all night, unable to take your eyes off the sky?

"How men would believe and adore," Emerson wrote, "and preserve for many generations the remembrance of the city of God which had been shown."

But the stars come out every night, and we don't look at them.

We must feed our muse a healthy diet of sense impression. We must absorb the world around us and learn to see that world anew, with eyes of childlike wonder. If we don't, when we try to describe, we'll have nothing but the words others have given us.

But the trouble is, as popular philosopher R.D. Laing observes, we don't notice that we don't notice. So we don't do anything about it.

To find out just how much you might be missing, try isolating one sense at a time. For example, find a safe spot outdoors, sit down, close your eyes and simply listen. You'll probably need a few moments to still the yammering from the infernal, internal receptionist, buzzing you with messages about all the Things You Should Be Doing. Ignore the ringing. It will stop.

Your very breath may betray you. I've discovered that as my mind races from one idea to the next, I often end up panting like an overheated schnauzer. I've had to relearn how to breathe in order to slow the mind's foolish careening. Concentrate on taking deep, slow breaths and letting them swell all the way down to the base of your spine. As breath slows, mind slows, and you become still.

As you do, you'll begin to hear things. First you'll note the familiar, expected sounds — crunch of shoes on gravel, hiss of tires on pavement. Don't try to find words to describe what you're hearing. Don't worry about remembering. Don't judge the nature or quality of the sounds. ("What an interesting noise." "What a melodious sound." "What a god-awful racket.") Just listen.

Gradually an undercurrent of sound will creep cautiously out from hiding — cicada hum from maple tree, gentle stirring of leaves, music so distant and so faint it could be memory, perhaps even the hollow hum of silence. Such sounds have been there all along, covered up by more assertive sounds and by your own brain babble. Only when you stop to listen will these other sounds emerge. Masking the dominant sense of sight heightens your sensitivity to them.

Here Comes "Old Dead Eye"

For Chuck Wheeler, such masking wasn't voluntary.

Chuck was an arresting sight when he filled my office door one afternoon. He's a big man, and his well-muscled torso attests to long sessions in the weight room. When I first saw him, he wore a full beard, dark glasses, scruffy jeans and a T-shirt bearing the legend "Here comes old dead eye."

Chuck had lost his sight in a boating accident. He'd had a difficult adjustment, and he was constructing a new life. He wanted to be a writer, and he had come to me for help.

As we sat in my office and talked about his work, I began to notice the extraordinary compensations nature had given Chuck to replace his sight.

"Ummm," he'd murmur. "Somebody's peeling an orange." (I'd later find out that the somebody was two halls over and behind a closed office door.)

"Hi, Cindy," Chuck would say as a student peeked in at the open office door but before she had said hello. He knew her by the sound of her footfall and the smell of her perfume. I hadn't even heard her coming and couldn't smell her at all, much less distinguish her from all the other students milling in the hallway.

This extraordinary sensitivity helped Chuck to become a powerful writer. I was delighted to watch his work become sharper and clearer and his voice more distinctive and assured.

Ten years later, and two thousand miles from the community college where Chuck and I worked together, I came across a review in the *New York Times Book Review* that brought back vivid memories. A first novelist had made an impressive debut with *Snakewalk*, the chronicle of a young man blinded in a boating accident. Chuck had written and published the book he had to write, and important folks had noticed.

I heard from Chuck recently. The screenplay for *Snakewalk* is finished, and he just sent novel number two to the agent. He has number three in progress, and several more are simmering. Nothing will stop him now, not even the marvelous success he is enjoying.

He isn't successful because he's blind. But he also hasn't let blindness stop him, and he uses his other senses to fully experience the world around him.

We don't need the "advantage" of blindness. We can wake up our senses by consciously changing the way we meet the world around us, by bringing a focused, intense concentration to our encounters.

Trading Earthquakes for Tornadoes

I find myself automatically concentrating in this way whenever I put myself into a new environment. I remember how strange everything seemed when I moved from Napa, California to Madison, Wisconsin. I had never seen yards without fences. I'd never heard a cicada. I'd never breathed air that was mostly water. I traded the sudden terror of an earthquake for the skin-prickling foreknowledge of a tornado. All was new, and I was as inquisitive and as open to life as a newborn.

Jogging became a daily adventure as I tried out new routes. I even stumbled and fell a couple of times because I was gawking at new sights, and my feet didn't know the way yet.

But newness faded. The comfort of familiarity embraced me. I could soon run without falling and find my way home without panic. But I paid for my security with loss of intensity and wonder.

To re-encounter that sense of newness and become scared and open again, I accept speaking engagements in faraway places. I enjoy the stimulation of new people with new ideas in Overland Park, Kansas or Pensacola, Florida. And I jog wherever I visit. That sense of newness refreshes me so.

I seek it in other ways: driving on country roads and meandering until I get lost, finding a new diner for breakfast, stopping at a country store to prowl the narrow aisles and hear the ancient floor creak underfoot.

You can meet the familiar world on unfamiliar terms. Leave for work early. Go a different route. Leave the car home and take the bike or—heresy of modern living—walk. Take what writer Natalie Goldberg calls an animal walk, absorbing all the sights and sounds and smells around you. Don't judge them. Accept them as gifts. Feel your body as it moves through air. Let your awareness spread gradually outward from yourself, to grass, trees and sky.

Seeing Tree Instead of Trees

You've seen trees all your life. Now concentrate on a specific tree. How is it different? Absorb it, without trying to write a mental description of it. Words about tree are not tree. Only tree is tree. And the specific tree before you now is like no other tree in the world.

Unlearn all you think you know about trees so that you can experience this tree. Don't let your concept of trees blind you to the real tree before you.

The tree is worthy of such attention. As Walt Whitman wrote: "A mouse is miracle enough to stagger sextillions of infidels."

As you devote your attention to the tree, you begin to notice small astonishments. The wind animates the leaves unevenly, the topmost a gentle rippling, the mid-section full of frenzy, the skirt almost still. The leaves are not simply green and yellow but dozens of variations of green and yellow, light and dark, sun and shade. The trunk, seen casually as a unified mass, becomes bumps and hollows, smooths and roughs. A gall on the bark signifies the presence of insects tapping into and altering the tree's genetic messengers.

Even this beginning description is hopelessly general. There aren't words enough or time to capture the complexity when you really experience the tree instead of trees.

Truly experience tree now and you will be able to describe tree in words later, as the picture re-forms in your mind. You can store many particular trees and choose the one tree your writing needs. Even if you want to write about trees in general, you can truly do so only by describing a particular tree, lovingly and accurately, just as it is.

If you don't really experience the tree, you'll have to resort to cliché when you try to describe it. What else will you have to work with but the tired words of others and the vague mental forms those words have created in your mind? But if you have absorbed the tree, you will be able to select carefully, using only those details that render the particular tree — or man or bicycle or toadstool or schnauzer — unique and that reinforce the impression you want to create.

If you give the reader a unique, specific portrait, your writing will be an experience of, not a statement about.

Create a Selective Sense Description

Try this experiment in perception and description. Select a person, animal or object and give it your total, intense, joyful attention for a few minutes (or as long as the experience gives you pleasure). Do it right now if you like.

Then get away from your subject and write down from memory as many details about it as you can. List anything that comes to mind. When you think you've exhausted your list, sit still for a few moments more, paper in lap, pencil in hand, and wait to see if more will come. (Often, you will do your best writing after you think you're finished.)

Now go back and compare the real dog or geranium or whatever to your list. Strike out the false, the pretentious, the self-important or precious, the stuff you wrote from your general sense of dog or geranium instead of from the actual experience.

Put your list down, close your eyes and picture your subject. What do you remember about it? How is it different from others of its kind? Use your list and your recollection to select only those two or three or four details that get at this uniqueness. Using just those details, write a description. Do it right now.

Were you able to stay out of the way of your description? It's not easy. Little mind wants to control, to shape the experience, to assert What It Knows. It will create little mind dog or little mind geranium, a hybrid one part reality to six parts self-importance. Only when you get out of the way and let the dog or geranium come through you will you begin to let the reader see what you see, experience what you experience, feel what you feel.

What a gift that is.

If your description is true to your vision, it will be unique and thus vivid. It can't be otherwise.

This is not self-expression. You're letting your subject express itself through you. Such writing isn't possible when the little mind insists on taking credit. But once the little mind lets go, such writing becomes almost effortless.

"The shot will only go smoothly," Eugene Herrigel writes in *Zen in the Art of Archery*, "when it takes the archer himself by surprise. You mustn't open the right hand on purpose."

The Wisdom in Getting out of the Way

Imagine being invited to an art exhibit. You sit in anticipation before the painting, which is veiled to heighten suspense. A critic appears and begins to describe the painting, telling you how beautiful it is, what she felt as she viewed it, what each detail means to her. And all the time you're burning with frustration. "Stop talking," you want to say. "Pull the sheet aside and let me see for myself."

Pull the sheet of controlling, judging ego-words aside. Let the reader see for herself.

When you write that way, you're saying that life itself matters. "The deepest secret in our heart of hearts," Goldberg says, "is that we are writing because we love the world."

When you embrace the details, you also embrace your reader, telling her, "You're worth the effort to get it right."

■ ■ ■ ■ ■ ■ ■ ■ ■ ■ ■ ■ ■
Interlude: The World of Auggie Wren

Author Paul Auster wrote of his incredible encounter with Auggie Wren, a man who has learned to pay attention.

According to Auster's account in the *New York Times*, Auggie Wren works behind the counter of a cigar store in downtown Brooklyn. But his true vocation is his art. Wren has filled twelve identical black photo albums with pictures taken at the corner of Atlantic Avenue and Clinton Street. When Auster first learned of the project, Wren had stood on that corner at exactly 7:00 a.m. every morning for twelve years and taken a color photo of the same view. When Auster saw the scrapbooks, there were over four thousand photographs of that one view.

The albums seemed at first "the oddest, most bewildering thing I had ever seen," Auster writes. All the pictures looked the same. What was the point? But as he continued to turn the pages, forcing himself to slow down and really look, Auster began to notice things: subtle shifts in the weather, in the angles of light, in the flow of traffic. He learned to tell weekdays from weekends, Saturdays from Sundays. He even began recognizing the faces of the passersby and to discover their different moods in the way they carried themselves day to day.

"Auggie was photographing time," Auster writes, "both natural time and human time, and he was doing it by planting himself in one tiny corner of the world and willing it to be his own."

In the same way, we can will our little chunk of the world to be our own and to capture it, not with a camera, but with words. By paying attention—intense, loving, careful attention—we can enrich our writing and make it real for the reader.

7

Nurturing and Nourishing Your Infant Ideas

You wouldn't send your baby to high school. And you wouldn't send your ten-year-old out to earn a living. So why send a child out to do a grown-up's job when it comes to your writing?

That's what you do when you ask an infant inspiration to do the work of a mature idea.

You must nurture and nourish your ideas until they mature. Just as with raising a child, you can't speed this maturation process. Sometimes you're not even aware of it as it occurs. But you can allow it to happen, by giving your ideas the time and the conditions necessary for healthy growth.

Embrace Your Babies

All this assumes, of course, that you're going to *have* ideas to nurture.

Actually, you're having them all the time. The trick is in recognizing and capturing them as they come. When you do that, you'll be reinforcing yourself for having the inspiration, and that will enable you to have even more of them.

If you haven't been aware of any great bubbling up of ideas from the subconscious, perhaps it's because you've been swatting your ideas away, treating them like petty annoyances.

"Not now! I'm working on something important."

Perhaps the receptionist isn't letting your ideas get through.

"I'm sorry. That line is busy. Would you care to hold?"

Or perhaps you aren't recognizing your ideas for what they are. You may be looking for a sonnet of rhyming couplets in iambic pentameter and may thus overlook the spark that could one day grow to become that sonnet. You're looking for a forest, and your subconscious is offering you a packet of seeds.

Or perhaps you're discounting your ideas simply because you're the one having them.

"If I thought of it, it can't be worth much."

If that's the case, you've got another squelcher to add to your list and learn to talk back to.

You must embrace your infant ideas and celebrate the subconscious process that gives birth to them.

Creativity on Demand—Almost

But you can go beyond simply embracing random inspiration as it occurs. You can prepare yourself to receive the inspirations you want, when you want them.

First, tell your subconscious what you'd like to produce. ("I want to write a sonnet that will express the delicate harmony between the human soul and the natural world that surrounds it.") Some folks write their goal on a slip of paper and carry it with them, taking it out to read it often. Others repeat the goal last thing before going to sleep each night. Even without such reminders, your subconscious will get the message. Don't try to tell your muse *how* to accomplish its miracles. You commission the work of art; leave the process up to the artist. And when the subconscious is ready, it will begin suggesting images, words, phrases, perhaps even a rhyming couplet or two.

Second, if you want to write a sonnet, eat, drink and sleep sonnets. If you want to write a humorous essay, devour humorous essays. If you want to write a romance novel, make romance novels your constant waking companions.

If you find a sonnet writer, humorist, or romance novelist that especially pleases you, adopt him or her as your mentor. Become a receptor of Shakespeare or Dave Barry or LaVyrle Spencer. Won't your ideas then be imitative of your mentor? At first, yes. But you'll soon find yourself thinking *like* your mentor, only *your* way. You'll learn form and you'll steal technique, but you'll develop your own voice. Your ideas will be your ideas.

As you begin to get those ideas, be open to them. Appreciate them—and appreciate yourself for having them. The best way to appreciate them is to pay attention to them. But be careful what form that attention takes.

Write It Down—But Don't Write Down Too Much, Too Soon

Fiction writer Richard Ford says he has carried a notebook around with him for twenty-five years and noted what he hears, "to remind myself that I'm a writer."

Follow Ford's lead and get in the habit of keeping a notebook with you all the time. Inspiration doesn't necessarily come when you're ready for it. It isn't a neat, orderly process. Accommodate yourself to the irregular workings of your muse. Keep open to suggestion twenty-four hours a day.

That means keeping a notebook or pad by the bed at night, too. Ideas may come to you under cover of darkness. They're not being bashful. You're just more likely to allow your big mind to play when your little mind has closed for the day, the chattering receptionist has gone home, and the switchboard has at last quieted down.

I learned this lesson the hard way. Years ago, a short story came to me, whole and perfect (it seemed to me at the time), in a waking dream in the middle of the night. Not wanting to leave the warmth and comfort of my bed to hunt down pencil and paper, I told myself I'd get up early and write the story. I rolled over and went back to sleep.

In the morning I awoke with the glorious feeling of certainty and beauty that had surrounded the dream-story. I remembered how wonderful the story had seemed. But I couldn't for the life of me remember the story. So far as I know, I never have.

Now I write down those stray nocturnal thoughts. When I get up in the morning and see what I've written, I sometimes find an illegible scrawl. Some of the ideas that presented themselves with such urgency turn out to be something less than earth-shaking ("Change the kitty litter"). But I've also received the occasional precious gift from the muse, including some ideas that I believe have helped this book a great deal, and these gifts make all the scribblings worth the effort.

When ideas come, day or night, note them just as they are. Don't try to shape or force them. Don't immediately try to convert the image into a poem, the scene into a play, the insight into an essay.

Write what you received, just as you received it.

This involves the same kind of concentration, receptivity and attention to detail we talked about earlier. Focus all of your energies on the notion itself. Don't worry about what it or you might become.

I'll give you four good reasons why:

1. If you try to impose shape and substance on your inspiration too soon, you may be wasting time and energy on an idea that will later prove to be a false start—one of the hundreds that writers receive, embrace and ultimately release in the course of developing their work.

2. Once you've invested time, energy and ego in an idea, you'll be more likely to want to hang onto it, good or not, and less likely to want or to be able to change it.

3. More important, you may stunt or distort the inspiration, changing its path so that, instead of reaching someplace new and exciting and imaginative, a place you've never been before, you force the idea to end up where you've already been.

4. And most important, by giving the inspiration specific form, you limit it to just one possibility. In its infant state, it can develop into many forms. The longer you wait, the more of these possibilities you'll be able to develop. Don't rush. There's time. You've captured the essence, so you needn't worry about forgetting. Now relax and let the subconscious continue to play. It's another case where there is much wisdom in waiting.

Wait to Judge, Too

As you receive these infant ideas, don't try to estimate their value. They are what they are. Receive them as such. Withhold judgment, positive or negative.

If you mentally move into the criticizing mode, letting little mind take over, you're moving out of the creating mode. The ideas will stop—even if the judgments you're making are positive. Note that point carefully.

Judging is self-conscious, the work of the aware ego. It isn't just negative judgment that will stop the flow of inspiration. *Any* judgment will do it.

I relearned this point most poignantly in a summer seminar I spoke at on the University of Wisconsin-Madison campus several years ago. I was sharing stories with writing teachers from all over the state. We were exploring ways to nurture creativity in the kids, and we of course landed on the subject of grading or otherwise judging their efforts.

A teacher told about the journal-writing exercise she developed for her fifth graders. She didn't read or grade their writing. She simply gave them time and encouraged them to write. Subject and form were entirely up to the young writers. Since there was to be no judgment, there could be no "mistakes."

I thought it a wonderful exercise and told her so. She agreed but was honest enough to report her one failure. One young man, she told us, refused to write. When writing time came, he would fold his arms and stare into space. He wasn't disruptive, and he was in other ways a cooperative and capable student. He just wouldn't play this particular game. Who knows why? Perhaps he thought writing was for sissies, or, worse, for girls. (You remember the age?) Perhaps he had been told that he was an awful writer. Perhaps he just didn't feel that he had anything to write about.

Whatever the reason, his wise teacher didn't force the issue. She let him stare while the others wrote.

Then one day, about halfway into a writing session, the young man took up his pencil, opened his notebook and began to write furiously. His need to express had become more compelling than his need not to write.

His teacher, quelling her impulse to turn cartwheels and light sparklers, moved quietly to the back of the room, leaned down over her new literary star and whispered, "Good for you," or words to that effect.

The boy immediately put down his pencil, closed his book, folded his arms and recommenced to stare.

The teacher was devastated.

She asked me why her student had reacted as he did. I didn't have an answer for her then, but I thought about the incident a lot, and later I shared this theory with her. Whatever was keeping the kid from writing was lodged in the conscious ego. When he finally began to write, he wrote from the subconscious, the true self, bypassing little mind and its non-writing self-image. He became lost in what he was writing. When his teacher praised him, she reminded him that he was writing. Little mind woke up, said, "We don't do this sort of thing!" and ordered the pencil down and the notebook shut.

Positive judgment can shut down creativity.

But negative judgment can be much more damaging.

You know the feeling when your hard work meets only indifference or outright criticism. From the meal you planned and cooked so carefully to the window trim you scraped and repainted with such attention to detail, you invest your self along with your sweat and your time. And that self can get hurt easily.

The hurt can be even greater with writing, because writing is often a more intimate sharing of self.

The hurt is greater still when the criticism hits the most sensitive and vulnerable part of our creative self, that shy elf who comes out of hiding to give you ideas and then scampers back into hiding again. Criticize my grammar; that's just something I *do* (or don't do). But criticize my idea or feeling, and you have passed judgment on who I *am*.

If the criticism is harsh enough, the hurt deep enough, the elf stays in hiding, and the gifts stop appearing.

Your own self-criticism of new ideas is not only hurtful. It's unfair. You've developed your critical standards by evaluating the published work of professional writers. If you use those standards to judge your infant idea, you're comparing your untested inspiration to ideas that have developed into writing that has been polished and published.

No wonder your baby doesn't seem to measure up.

The fact is, you can't judge your ideas effectively as you're receiving them anyway. You get all tangled up emotionally in the process of having the idea, and you can't tell a good one from a bad one.

And good or bad for what? Perhaps the inspiration won't work out for the project you're grappling with now, but it might be perfect for the project you don't even know you're going to be working on later. (Maybe the subconscious knows and just hasn't told the rest of you yet.)

There's no statute of limitations on an idea's potential usefulness. The idea you jot down today may serve the work you're writing tomorrow or may become the basis for the work you'll be doing next week. But you might not find the other pieces of that particular puzzle for a month, a year, even a decade. Be patient with your notions.

My grandfather was a professional writer for all his adult life. He always jotted down his stray inspirations in a notebook. One day a title came to him: "The Left-Handed House." He waited, but nothing more came. He noted the title and went on to other things.

Fully twenty years later, he wrote the story that went with the title and published it in the *Saturday Evening Post*.

The Wisdom of Forgetting

You're not going to be able to write down every idea. You're going to lose some. It's inevitable. But that's okay. You don't *have* to write down every idea.

You're going to have more wonderful ideas than you can use in fifteen lifetimes. And the really good ones, the ones that you were put here to write, will keep coming back.

In fact, there's a certain wisdom in forgetting. Suppose an idea dashes or dithers across your consciousness, and you fail to note it. One of two things will happen. You may forget the idea entirely, and it's lost to you. But if an idea can't keep you interested in the courtship stage, chances are you weren't going to develop a long and happy marriage anyway.

The idea may come back. If it does, it's likely to have become stronger, sharper, clearer. "Get a load of me now," it seems to say. "Bet you can't ignore me again."

Suppose you do. Again, you may forget. But the notion may come knocking on your mental door a third time. This time it's no child. It's a powerful, swaggering adolescent, no longer crying for attention but demanding it. You'll deal with this arrogant youth now or it's likely to steal your car keys and take off on its own.

Trust yourself and trust the process. The ideas you really need to have are going to use you to get expressed.

What to Do on Judgment Day

As exhilarating as receiving and noting your inspirations can be, it isn't enough. Perhaps you know a frustrated would-be writer who fills notebook after notebook with notions, has scraps of paper peeking out of pockets and overflowing tabletops, but who never actually gets around to writing any of the creations those ideas might have become.

As a disciplined, productive writer, you'll need to cull your scrap heap regularly, looking for workable ideas.

When it's time to evaluate and act on your inspiration, remember to play the angel's advocate first. Instead of trying to decide what's wrong with an idea, first note everything that's right with it, everything it might become, all the possibilities it might suggest. Good ideas come from having lots of ideas.

Don't be afraid to stray from the original inspiration. It may simply be the signpost to lead you down a new path. In this way, you'll spread out from your initial starting point.

After you've spread out, dig deep. Don't settle for the idea as it first came to you. Develop other ways to say the same thing. There's no right way to express an idea. Look for what creativity guru Roger von Oech calls "the second right answer," and then look for the third and the fourth. You'll have a better chance of finding what you need if you explore many possibilities. Playing with language in this way may lead you to better ways to express your initial vision, and it may also lead you to new visions.

■ ■ ■ ■ ■ ■ ■ ■ ■ ■ ■ ■ ■ ■ ■ ■ ■ ■
Interlude: What Tootle Taught Me About Writing

With apologies to Robert Fulghum, I think we already know a lot by the time we get to kindergarten.

In fact, just about everything I ever needed to know I learned from Horton, Ferdinand and Tootle.

From Dr. Seuss's wonderful elephant, Horton, I learned not only the value of but the nobility in being faithful — 100 percent, no matter what — to your promises and commitments.

Munro Leaf's passivist bull, Ferdinand, taught me a more subversive lesson, perhaps the most important lesson of all: You must be yourself. Hamlet's father only said it. Ferdinand *lived* it — and suffered the consequences. It's okay for a bull to sit under a cork tree and smell the flowers — even if it means disappointing the crowd that expects you to butt and snort and gore matadors instead.

And from Gertrude Crampton's dear Tootle, the train, I learned another subversive lesson—that there are great joys awaiting us when we stray off the tracks and into the fields. I don't think that was the message Crampton meant to convey. As I remember, the townsfolk use red flags to train Tootle to stay *on* the track. But it really isn't for the author to say what lesson a reader may draw.

Apply these lessons to your writing. If you aren't 100 percent faithful to your inspiration, you may give up on an idea—and yourself—before it really had a chance to develop. If you write only what others say is okay for you to write, you may never learn to write your own truth. And if you only explore the story you have outlined, you miss the stories you might have discovered had you wandered off the tracks.

I apparently absorbed something from Tibor Gergely's illustrations for Tootle, too. I've already told you how strange and scary life seemed when my wife, son and I moved to the Midwest from California. We landed in Madison, Wisconsin for my wife's job interview during one of the worst winters on record. Had we landed on the moon instead, the landscape could hardly have seemed more alien, more uninhabitable.

And yet, as a realtor drove us out to the neighboring town of Stoughton to show us houses, I felt as if I were coming home after a long trip. The landscape seemed not only familiar but comforting and somehow right. I felt as if I belonged.

I can't explain this. Nothing in my past could have prepared me for the rolling fields and small towns of Wisconsin. I was a Southern California kid, full of freeways, beaches and smog. What did I know about cows?

My father spent much of his childhood on a truck farm in upstate New Jersey. Could he have somehow conveyed a sense of that place to me as a child, so that, years later, I seemed to recognize and be drawn to a land I had never seen before? Maybe, but Dad had an awful childhood, and I'm sure he never talked about it until I was much older, and then never in nostalgic terms.

Maybe I came with this sense of familiarity and kinship to a place built in, part of the Marshall template. How else to explain other seemingly "natural" inclinations, my love of writing and of newspapers, for example, which I'm pretty sure predated my ability to read? My family says I "got it" from my grandfather Beymer. I bear an uncanny facial resemblance to him, undoubtedly passed along in the DNA. But could I have also inherited a defining passion? Is it a part of the genetic code, along with having blue eyes and being color-blind and ambidextrous?

I don't know. I can't explain it. And I can't explain the fact that the first time I saw the girl who would one day be my wife, my soul stirred as if recognizing its mate. Was that programmed into the DNA, too?

I can't explain any of this. But I want to bring it all along with me when I write — and not to limit myself to the part of me that little mind can explain and name and control.

Like Tootle, I want to plunge off the tracks and write about the fields, too, which brings me to the Tootle Theory to explain my instant sense of belonging in the Midwest. Maybe Tootle created in me a sense of place that is just as strong and real to me as my remembrance of the neighborhood where I grew up. Maybe the countryside between Madison and Stoughton brought me back to the countryside that Tootle traveled when he jumped off the track.

Everything you've ever experienced is inside you, waiting to be set free in your writing. When you touch it, you are touching your truth. When you write from this truth, you are being creative in the most fundamental way possible.

Maybe, then, your Muse, your Creativity, is nothing more and nothing less than your Truth, the all of you that you have been a lifetime creating.

Play the "What If?" Game

In a recent episode of Dik Browne's delightful "Hi and Lois" comic strip, Hi and his young son are watching the golf match on television. "What if they played golf underwater?" the youngster asks, and then, because one question leads to another, "What if the sand traps were filled with snakes?" and "What if they played golf on the moon? With bowling balls?"

We need to call upon the child in us to ask the kind of "what if?" questions that can enrich our creations and lead us to new ones.

I began a short story with an image: a husband and wife driving cross-country in separate cars, moving their belongings and them-selves to a new home. I played "What if?" with the scene. What if they became separated? A fine editor, the late Dan Curley of *Ascent* magazine, pushed me further by rejecting the first two endings I came up with. He led me to a final "What if?": What if the separation was intentional, an unhappy wife's creative way of escaping a mar-riage? That last "What if?" led me to write my only award-winning short story, "Le Gran Naranja."

By maintaining this kind of receptivity and playfulness, you'll soon have dozens of maturing ideas. As they ripen, they'll also begin suggesting the shape and form they must take. If you're interested in publishing what you write, you'll also be thinking about possible markets for the creations these ideas can become.

But often you'll need more than what's already in your head to turn your inspiration into a fully developed idea and then into a completed work of fiction or nonfiction. You'll need to do some research.

Does that sound horribly uncreative? As we'll see in the next chapter, you can and should bring your openness and your willing-ness to take chances to this vital step in the writing process.

8

Creative Gathering

In chapter six we talked about ways to develop an eager openness to the world around us. This absorbing of sense impression may serve no immediate, practical purpose. You're not likely to come home from an animal walk and dash off a salable piece about the experience. But you'll store those sense impressions in your subconscious, and the bits and scraps of your world will reemerge when you need them in your writing—one of the many great gifts your muse gives you.

We turn now to a kind of gathering with more immediate, tangible benefits. This purposeful gathering includes library research, interviewing and a regular mining of the media.

You can apply a creative approach to each step in the writing process, including those steps grouped under the term "research." You'll want to apply the same openness and the same intensity here as you would to every other step in the writing process.

Creativity seems to thrive best in an environment of abundance or even excess. Gather much more than you'll ever actually use in your writing. That way, you can select from among quotations, descriptions, anecdotes and ideas. The extra material, even though it doesn't appear in the finished writing, will strengthen every paragraph you write.

You might compare the process of researching your subject to casting a play. Suppose you have three major rolls to cast for your production of *A Streetcar Named Desire*—the swaggering brute, Stanley Kowalski; his long-suffering wife, Stella; and Stella's fading sister, Blanche. Let's further suppose that three actors respond to your casting call—skinny, anemic Phil; eager, unseasoned Ted and adequate but unexciting Marla. You have a warm body to fill each role, all right, but Phil will make an awfully scrawny and ultimately unconvincing Stanley, you'll have to put a wig on Ted so he can play Stella, and Marla just doesn't have the umph to utter the immortal line "I have always relied on the kindness of strangers" with much conviction.

Your production will be something less than an artistic triumph.

But if thirty eager men and women show up for auditions, your chances of finding an appropriate, reasonably talented actor for each part will be greatly increased, and you'd have understudies to fill in just in case.

In the same way, if you have ten times more information than you can use for your writing, you'll come to understand your subject better during "auditions," and the material you do put on stage will be the best possible for the part.

Some projects may require relatively little gathering, because you have all or most of the materials at hand from your life experience (as with a reminiscence or a highly autobiographical short story, for example). Other projects may require enormous research (an article assignment on a subject about which you know nothing).

If you don't do enough gathering, your budding project will suffer from malnutrition (we've shifted from the stage to the kitchen for our metaphor) and will grow up stunted. It might even die. You just can't write around a lack of information. I find that when I try, my writing gets fancier and fancier, the sentences longer and longer, the words further and further removed from everyday speech. But I'm just tatting around the black hole. The void remains. This isn't writer's block. It's writer's blank. And there's a simple cure. Go back and get the information you need to make your writing work. (I find it's often true that when I'm having trouble with one stage of the writing, I need to go back a step to solve the problem. Is it that way for you, too? See chapter nine for more ideas on dealing with writer's block.)

But you can overdo research if you allow it to become an excuse for putting off that confrontation with the blank page or screen. You can always read another book or interview another source. But do you need to?

Wrong question. Does the writing need it? Learn to ask that question; answer it as honestly as you can. Then get on with it (using the start-up techniques we'll talk about in chapters eleven and twelve).

Everyone Has an Uncle Who Worked for the Circus

In the gathering stage, tell your friends, colleagues and casual acquaintances what you're working on. Now's no time for coyness or secrecy. Why? Because that friend or acquaintance just might have an uncle who used to work for the circus (or play on a minor league baseball team, or work in retail sales, or suffer from coronary disease, or whatever subject you're currently exploring). Everyone has stories to tell, information to share, names to offer.

Two examples from my own work experience:

My first assignment for *Wisconsin Trails* was in fact to write about the circus. I was pretty excited, thinking I'd get to travel around the state all summer, attending circuses. Wrong. I got to look at slides of last summer's circus and write a piece from that.

Being new and especially eager to please, I over-researched, gathering not ten times but one hundred times more than I could ever use. I read articles and books on circus, studied circus posters, went to the nearby Circus World Museum and in general immersed myself in circus. (I think my pay for this article worked out to about five cents an hour.)

But none of this research paid off near so well as a comment I happened to make to my friend and colleague, Blake Kellogg. When I mentioned circus, he lit up like the "tilt" sign on a pinball machine. Turns out he's a true circus fanatic, at that time a member of the Board of Directors of the State Historical Society (which runs Circus World Museum) and one of the country's foremost experts on circus carousel horses. He told me wonderful stories about the circus. I used some of what he told me in the article, used more to direct my thinking and research, let the rest simply inform and strengthen my task. Because of his help, I wrote with confidence and conviction.

I learned a lesson from this encounter. I began inflicting my projects on just about everybody, including those who come to hear me speak at writers conferences. When I spoke in Overland Park, Kansas, for example, I was researching an article and a short story on radio on-air personalities. (They don't like to be called disc jockeys any more.) I mentioned this during my morning presentation. At the noon break, a member of the audience came up, shook my hand and announced that he had been a drive-time DJ in the Kansas City market for years, and did he have some stories for me! Over lunch he gave me material I probably never would have found anywhere else.

Roam the Back Pages of the Press

I also mine the media for material, and you should, too. I graze the front pages, of course, but it's often the back-page fillers and features that spark me.

The process works in three ways. First, something in the media may translate directly into a new story or article idea. When I read about the plight of Clayton Moore, for example, a story began growing inside me. Moore, you may remember, was TV's Lone Ranger for years. After the series ran its wonderful course ("Return with us now to those thrilling days of yesteryear"), Moore continued to appear in mask and white hat at supermarket parking lots around the country, performing his fast draw and talking with the kids about loving their country and obeying their parents.

But when the wide-screen spectacular version of The Lone Ranger hit the theaters, with a younger actor in the title role, a judge ruled that Moore could no longer wear the mask he had made famous and that continued to give him a sense of identity and purpose. The public might be confused, the judge said.

The story angered and touched me. I was — okay, still am — a big Lone Ranger fan. I could identify with Moore's plight. In my mind and heart, he still was and always would be the Lone Ranger. That's why my spirit sang when I read that Moore was continuing to play the Ranger, without the forbidden mask but with dark, wrap-around glasses — a triumph of spirit and ingenuity over the letter of the law.

I wrote "Willard and the Rider" based on Moore's experience, and I still think it's one of the best short stories I've done.

Media grazing can help out with an idea in progress, too. When I'm working on a particular project, I notice that stories about the subject seem to jump out at me from the newspapers and magazines I read. They were probably there all the time; I just never noticed them until I needed them. When I do notice them, I clip them and put them in folders labeled by subject. From these clips I get ideas, up-to-date information and a richer understanding of my subject. Although I obviously wouldn't lift any quotes from stuff that has already appeared in print under someone else's byline, I do note names of sources I can call to generate new quotes and anecdotes.

I also cull the print media for stories relating to a number of interests I've maintained for years. For example, I have a huge folder on "cowboys," another on "cafés and diners," a third on "stories from the blue highways," a fourth on "life in small-town U.S.A." I keep folders on the late rock singer Ricky Nelson, on master story-teller Garrison Keillor, on author Ken Kesey. I've got a couple of file drawers full of these folders, which comprise my personal reference library, open twenty-four hours a day, three hundred sixty-five days a year. Sometimes I'll browse through a folder, hoping that old articles will spark new ideas. They often do. And when they don't, I thoroughly enjoy myself anyway.

I have three thick folders on minor league baseball. I've occasionally drawn on these materials for magazine articles. I'm now using them for that novel I'm writing on a minor league baseball team called the Beymer Bisons. (You're going to hear more about this later on.)

I've got piles of stuff on our local Class A team, the Madison Muskies, starting with a program from their first home game and going through (so far) articles on the likelihood that current ownership will sell the team or move it to another city (and break my poor heart in the process).

I've got tons of statistics, the blood and sinew of baseball. Did you know, for example, that Joe Bauman has the all-time record for most home runs in a season, seventy-two in 1954 for Roswell? I thought not. Or that the most lopsided game in modern baseball history occurred in the Texas League on June 15, 1902 when Corsicana buried Texarkana, 51-3? You could look it up—in my clip file.

But it's the anecdotes that have truly goosed my creative muse and gotten me started on my baseball novel.

Item. The Vancouver Canadians forfeited their July 6, 1989 game with the Albuquerque Dukes of the Pacific Coast League because players' salary checks didn't arrive in time.

Item. Mal Fichman, manager of the Boise Hawks, returned to the diamond dressed in the costume of the team mascot after being ejected from the game for protesting a series of calls.

Item. Eight men were tossed out of a July 4, 1989 game between Midland Angels and the Wichita Wranglers. Among the banished miscreants was the Midland public-address announcer, who played Linda Ronstadt's "When Will I Be Loved?" ("I've been cheated, been mistreated . . .") over the PA to protest an umpire's call.

Item. The Quad City Angels returned to their locker room after dropping a tough game to discover that police had seized their equipment because of an unpaid hotel bill.

Most of these incidents will find their way into my novel, and they've all helped shape the mood and tone along with the plot of the book.

In fact, I'll bet that the long piece I read and clipped about the plight of Little Falls, New York after it lost its beloved baseball team, the Little Mets, helped plant the notion that later grew into my central plot-line: will Beymer keep the Bisons, despite low attendance and a crumbling ballpark?

Clip files don't always turn into novels. But they can supply ideas, inspiration and energy for your writing.

Mix Business With Pleasure

You can and should be gathering creatively when you read for fun, too. For example, suppose you enjoy the novels of Elmore Leonard. (He's on my mind just now, as I'm reading a lot of his stuff to get ready to hear him speak at an upcoming writers' conference.) His tense plots and tight characterization carry you away from the cares and concerns of life. You lose track of time. The mood stays with you for days.

All well and good. But you can also read as a writer, not just for enjoyment, but for ideas, inspiration and instruction. Would you steal the plot of *Killshot* for a suspense novel of your own? I suspect not, since your sense of ethics would probably forbid it, and because no publisher wants another *Killshot* after Leonard did such a nifty job on the first one. But could *Killshot* spark your own plot ideas? Sure. Almost all plots are derivative. Shakespeare never developed an original plot line. But he sure did a lot with the ones he borrowed.

And chances are, if you like to read a certain type of novel, for example, you'd probably like to write that type of novel as well. Contrarily, trying to force yourself to write a suspense novel if you can't quite bring yourself to actually read one doesn't make a lot of sense. You'd have a lousy time, and you probably wouldn't do a very good job of it.

A writer as good as Leonard can also teach us much about the craft of writing. If his scenes seem especially vivid and well-focused to you, as they do to me, try to figure out why. You'll soon discover that Leonard always renders a scene from the point of view of one of the involved characters. That way, every scene has an attitude. It's a wonderful technique.

As an apprentice magician, you can't be satisfied with enjoying the magic show. You must try to sneak backstage to find out how the trick is done. Unlike magicians, writers can't hide their tricks. Technique is right there for you to study.

I used to worry that such study would ruin the enjoyment of reading, but I haven't found that to be the case. I'll sometimes read good material twice, once for enjoyment and content, once for craft. What I learn in the process seems to make me even better able to enjoy the next reading encounter.

Cast your net widely as you read. Pursue new work by old-favorite authors, certainly, and read deeply in the subjects that interest you. But seek out new favorites, too, and let one subject suggest another. I "discovered" Larry McMurtry (about ten years after the rest of the world, apparently) when I read a piece in which Ken Kesey (one of my favorite writers) said that he read and admired McMurtry very much. I figured I couldn't want a better recommendation than that, and I haven't regretted a minute of the time I've spent with McMurtry (who is now another of my favorite writers).

Don't Check Your Creativity at the Library Door

Do you have a hard time putting the words "library," "research" and "creative" into the same sentence? You shouldn't. Mining library sources is really creative sleuthing. If an initial search of the card catalog and the *Reader's Guide to Periodical Literature* turns up nothing, you've encountered a creative opportunity, one of those moments when the easy answer doesn't work.

Bring your creative attitude of flexibility and openness to this moment. If you can't find what you're looking for under one subject listing, spend a few minutes brainstorming all the possible categories your subject might appear under. Do the same thing with reference volumes. If you can't find your subject in the *Who's Who*, might he or she be hiding in another, more specialized volume?

Play detective. Let one clue lead to another. The hunt can be especially exhilarating if your library has replaced that card catalog (don't those rows of drawers look like a morgue for midgets?) with computers. They speed up the process and help you to make new connections, the essence of the creative process.

Be ready to find what you're not looking for. In the initial stages of research, you might not know enough to know what you don't know. Be open to happy surprises. As in the process of writing for discovery, you can use research as a tool of discovery, too. One name or fact or insight, even a seemingly irrelevant one, can lead to another that's right on target.

Finally, don't forget that living, breathing resource sitting at the desk behind the sign that reads "reference librarian." This expert on learning how to learn can save you a lot of wander-around time and point you in directions you hadn't anticipated.

The Hunt for That First Name

For a great deal of the work I do—nonfiction magazine articles—I rely on firsthand or primary sources rather than secondary or print sources. I'll use my clip files and library research as a starting point, but I must develop material that has never been in print before.

But often I start an assignment with a subject, perhaps even a slant or angle, but no names of people to talk to. Another creative challenge. I must find that crucial first name, a person who can give me some of the information I need and, even more important, point me toward other sources.

If you find yourself in this situation, first comb your print sources for likely names. Articles and books often cite sources that can be helpful to you, and the fellow who wrote the article or book can become an interview source. Track these folks down through an agent or publisher, if necessary, but often you can get a phone number by simply calling information for the person's city. Many have listed numbers, and even the ones with answering machines, secretaries, spouses or other effective screening devices will often return your calls with a wonderful willingness to share information.

Like a good reporter, you should develop a beat list—names and numbers of sources you've dealt with in the past. I often begin my search by calling a few of my workhorse sources, who include university professors, reporters, local business people and friends with exotic hobbies.

If print sources and your beat list don't get you started, try the nearest university or college news, information or public relations service and ask, "Do you have any experts on . . . ?" And once again, don't forget your good friend the reference librarian.

You'll be exposing your ignorance to the world. But you'll soon learn that the only truly stupid question is the question you don't ask, out of shyness or ego or whatever.

Be Ready for Surprises When You Interview

You'll sometimes have to go into an interview cold, knowing little about your subject and even less about the person you hope will enlighten you. This isn't all bad. Sometimes your ignorance will evoke pity and an outpouring of helpful information.

But by failing to prepare, you run the risk of offending your subject with an ignorant or insensitive question ("Gee, Ms. Steele, don't you write novels or something?"), of failing to ask the right questions and of failing to understand what your source tells you.

As a consequence, you should always try to prepare for an interview — by reading about your subject and the subject matter and by talking to the subject's colleagues. Then build a list of questions. When I started out, I wrote the questions, usually on a stiff, 5 × 9 card, which I could keep in my lap or on the table next to my notepad. That way I was sure to remember what I wanted to ask. My list kept me on track and also helped me to relax. Now, several hundred interviews later, I generally formulate the questions in my mind, often on the way to the interview.

I've learned to perform another ritual of preparation that I've found to be extremely helpful. I used to let the disaster tapes roll in my mental movie house (you know the movies I mean: "I Was a Tongue-tied Interviewer," "Brain-dead Interviewer From Outer Space," "The Man Who Spilled Coffee on His Pants"). They did a wonderful job of making me tense and squeaky-voiced, and they probably helped to call forth the awful realities I most feared (like tied tongues and stained pants).

Now I visualize the interview going exactly as I want it to be. I see myself calm, assured, friendly, natural. I ask my questions respectfully, listen intently. My subject is forthright and engaging. We have a productive conversation, with my subject doing almost all of the talking. We part with a warm handshake and the subject's assurance that I can call back anytime for more information or to clarify any point.

Not every interview goes perfectly, of course. I still have my share of hostile witnesses and Gary Coopers ("Yep. Nope.") But I find myself much more calm and assured after a bit of positive visualization, and I'm better able to handle the rough spots when I encounter them.

As important as such preparation is, often the best moments in an interview contain surprises, and my best questions aren't the ones I made up in advance. The best questions come in response to what I'm hearing. This can only happen when I'm really listening, intensely and actively, making sense out of what I'm hearing, asking for clarification when I can't make sense, making sure I understand what my subject is saying and implying.

As we noted in chapter six, creativity involves receptivity. This is especially true in creative interviewing. You must open up to absorb your subject's words. When you do, the subject will respond by providing more and better information, insight, self-revelation. Listening is a great gift we too-seldom give. If you don't believe me, go to a local rest home and see if you can find someone willing to tell you a story or two about his or her life. Really listen to what you get. You'll have a tough time escaping with anything short of a full, rich personal history.

We so often define creativity in terms of self-expression. But creative interviewing involves a determined effort not to express too much self, not to talk too much at all. Certainly you can react to what you hear, can tell a story in order to get a story back. But your ego must vanish as you subordinate your own knowledge and the natural desire to appear intelligent to a sincere desire to understand the other.

You must also be absolutely open about your ignorance. Don't bluff. Don't be afraid to say, "I don't understand" and "Could you explain that to me?" and "Would you give me an example?" Your ability to learn derives from such ignorance. Again, the only really foolish question is the one you didn't ask for fear of appearing foolish.

With practice, this kind of intense listening will become not only natural but intensely pleasurable as you watch another human being unfold and reveal self to you.

And later on, when you sit down to write, you'll experience the even more pleasurable sensation of having wonderful material with which to write.

I have found that any subject, from the media-savvy pro to the shy neophyte, has a good story to tell and will open up if we only ask the right questions and then really listen to the answers.

I once interviewed Bernie Little, owner of the fastest hydroplane in the world, the Miss Budweiser. I met Little in his mobile coach on the shores of the Detroit River, where the Miss Budweiser was racing. I had prepared carefully, reading up on Little and on hydroplane racing, one of many subjects about which I know nothing. I also received a last-minute tip from Little's publicist, Bonnie Anderson. "Ask him about his grandchildren," she told me as I mounted the steep steps into the lavish home on wheels that served as Little's office.

Little was cordial and articulate. A pro at being interviewed, he was able to recite almost word-for-word the anecdotes I had already encountered in the press clippings I had read for background. I wasn't getting anything new, and I knew the folks at *The Yacht* magazine, who had paid my air fare to meet with Little, weren't getting anything approaching their money's worth.

Too soon, Little was standing, hand extended, practiced smile in place, indicating that the interview was over. He had me three-quarters out the door when I remembered to blurt out a question about his grandchildren.

Before I fully realized what had happened, I was back in my chair across from Little, a fresh Diet Coke in my hand, while Little poured out forty-five minutes worth of personal anecdotes I hadn't found in any press kit.

That "boring" employee-of-the-month you have to write a profile on isn't really boring at all. You just haven't asked the right question yet, the one about the grandkids, or the model train layout in the basement, or the collection of ships-in-a-bottle, or the country western songs she writes as a hobby.

Keep asking, and keep listening. It's all part of the creative process of feeding your muse.

And approach every research task with a creative attitude of openness to possibility.

9

Creative Procrastination

Have you noticed that for every adage, there is an equal and opposite adage?

"The one who hesitates is lost," folk wisdom decrees, but "Act in haste. Repent in leisure."

So for a writer, which is it? Should you grit your teeth, push through that block, write til it hurts and hurt til it writes? Or should you wait for the guidance of inspiration, wait until the writing "feels good," thus giving your subconscious time to simmer and sift and yield its insight.

The answer is an emphatic and unequivocal "It depends."

Sometimes it's easy to find reasons for putting off that eternal wrestling match with the written word. When the words don't seem to want to come, we always have more pleasant things we could be doing (like clipping the cat's claws or cleaning the gunk off the lawn mower blades).

We know we must fight the urge to procrastinate. 'Tis nobler to affix your backside to the chair and hack your way through the tangle. The Nike® shoe ads have it right: "Just do it!"

And yet—there's wisdom, too, in the notion that creativity can't be forced and that true insight often appears in the silences, the in-betweens.

How can we reconcile these two contrary bits of wisdom? How are we to know when we're creatively waiting and when we're simply stalling?

A lot depends on knowing yourself and your unique way of approaching your writing. For some, procrastination presents a serious problem. You may be constantly battling what you've learned to call "writer's block." (We really should have more than one name for it; I'm sure there are almost as many kinds of "writer's block" as there are blocked writers.) If so, you'll want to pay special attention to the chapters dealing with getting started. The tricks in these chapters will help you blast through your blocks.

Take a Giant Step Backwards

And you'll also want to keep this tip in mind: If you're stuck at any stage in the creative process, go back one step to find your solution. If you can't seem to get those first words to flow, take a step back and organize your thoughts. If you're having trouble organizing, retreat to the research stage and gather more information. If you don't yet know what you're looking for, go all the way back to step one and think through your purpose. If you don't feel ready for a step, you're probably not, and that benevolent stranger in your subconscious is trying to tell you so.

But don't, whatever you do, mistake the apparent block for a signal to bail out all together. You must recognize the reason for the block and work your way through it. Do this today, and it will be easier to do it tomorrow. Get in the habit, and soon the blocks will disappear.

The next time you find yourself engrossed in a wonderful piece of writing, know that the writer probably battled through several blocks and a couple of dark nights of the soul to get those words to you in finished form.

Creative Procrastination: Inducing Writer's Block

But not all of us are procrastinators. If you're like me, you may have the opposite problem. I'm the kind of writer who can't wait to get to the word processor, put my fingers on the keys and see what appears on the screen. I'm not saying that the product is always wonderful (as you well know by now). And I'm not saying my work doesn't need as much revision and editing as anybody else's. But I love to write, and I usually can't wait to get at it.

You procrastinators may be envious, but my eagerness is a mixed blessing. Often I'll rush a project, getting it into what I imagine to be final form without waiting so see what else my subconscious might have had to say about it and without giving myself enough time to develop all the possibilities.

That's precisely why I'm often most creative when I get stuck, when the right answer doesn't present itself immediately, when my fingers don't know which keys to push next. These moments force me to look at the problem from a different angle. As little mind struggles, rails, quits in frustration, big mind often takes over, plays with the problem and presents me with not one but a variety of possible solutions.

After years of rushing, I've learned to build a bit of a block into the process at times. Rather than fearing writer's block, I actually induce it by employing what I call "creative procrastination."

These self-induced blocks come in two varieties: the "do-nothing" and the "do-something-different."

The Do-nothing Block

I'm writing the trial run for this chapter on a Monday morning. (If you don't like what you're reading, blame it on that.) As Monday's go, this one's a beauty, a real coming-of-fall heart-wrencher, complete with blue skies and gentle breezes off the lake.

I was ready to write this chapter last Friday, but I put it off until today—not because I didn't want to write it but because I want it to be as good as I can make it. I figured a little creative procrastination might help.

Sometimes it pays to put a little space between you and your inspiration. As you develop your ideas and gather your materials, hold off drawing conclusions and imposing structure for as long as you can. Let your subconscious create and suggest possibilities.

Such withholding may generate considerable anxiety. When the words aren't marching across the page, you may begin to feel that they never will. One successful writer—with hundreds of articles and several books behind him—told me he still feels sure each time he approaches a new project that words will literally fail him and he'll have nothing to say.

Such fears are natural. They may even be universal among writers. Put them to work for you as creative energy. Just as a public speaker harnesses the butterflies and gets them to fly in formation, converting natural anxiety into attentiveness and focus, you can use the heightened awareness and sensitivity that come with anxiety to help you be a better writer. Here's how.

First, make a date to create. Set a specific time and place. I was ready to write on Friday, but I marked my mental calendar for Monday morning, 8:00 a.m., office.

Then put the project out of your mind and let the anticipation build. Each time the words begin to form in your mind, send them away. Let the notion simmer in your subconscious. It may emerge stronger, more fully formed, more richly detailed.

Meanwhile, do a little mental drifting. Do hang gliding through your mental skies. Engage in what writer Dorothea Brande calls "wordless recreation." Listen to classical music. Take in a baseball game (my favorite wordless recreation by far). Sand the porch (my current least-favorite but most pressing wordless recreation). Weed the garden. Whatever you do, get away from words.

You'll emerge refreshed and eager to write. The well of words will refill without your being aware of the quiet change in the level. You and your idea will be ready for writing. You'll attack the project with renewed vigor, and your subconscious may provide you with insights you didn't know you had.

But what happens if you're seized with inspiration before the appointed time? What, for example, if this chapter had wanted to flow out of me on Sunday morning at 3:00 a.m.?

I would have leapt out of bed, grabbed a pen and a pad of paper and done my best to keep up with my runaway writing. If you find yourself on the tiger's back, ride that tiger until you and it are exhausted. Capture every word. You've created inspiration; it just arrived a little ahead of schedule. You dare not ignore it.

(That happy exaltation didn't occur for me on this chapter, but I'll bet the work is just as good for having come in trickles rather than torrents.)

And what happens if you show up at the appointed time, and inspiration stands you up? Write anyway. Make a beginning. Put something down and see what happens next. Chances are you'll be able to write yourself into your material and into your inspiration.

The Do-something-different Block

A few chapters back, I warned that I'd be taking you to a town called Beymer, Wisconsin, before this book was done. Now's the time.

I first discovered Beymer in my subconscious almost ten years ago. So far as I can tell, it's a combination of the little Southern California town I grew up in (back when "little town" and "Southern California" weren't mutually exclusive) and several towns I've visited or driven through since moving to Wisconsin. I wrote a series of short stories about Beymer as I imagined it would have been in 1957. The stories all centered on Bruce Kelly, editor of the weekly Beymer *Banner*. I published a couple of the stories, won an "honorable mention" in a literary contest for a collection of the Beymer stories, and put the project away.

But my subconscious evidently snuck off to Beymer to visit from time to time. So when the notion to write a novel about a minor league baseball team faced with extinction began to bubble in my brain, it suddenly became clear to me that I would be going back to Beymer for my fictional setting.

Plot and setting came easily. I've been following minor league baseball all my life, and I've collected lots of stories. I know what a minor league ballpark feels like before, during and after a game, and I've felt the desolation of tromping through the snow where an outfield used to be.

I knew how the book should begin, and I knew in general terms what direction it would take. I didn't know for sure how it would end, but I've learned not to let that bother me. It's more fun to discover as you go along.

I was ready to write. Or so I thought. Except that every time I tried, the stuff came out stiff. I wasn't having any fun, and I figured a reader probably wouldn't have any either.

I tried "do-nothing procrastination." It didn't work. I did nothing, and nothing happened. Actually, I did quite a bit, including writing another book called *Writing for the Joy of It*. If you're going to engage in creative procrastination, but you're dependent on your writing to earn or supplement your grocery money, you'd better get in the habit of keeping several projects going at once.

I mean to say that I did nothing on the novel. I kept listening for voices from Beymer, but all I heard was silence.

I suppose I could have discarded the project. I've had my share of false starts. But the project wouldn't leave me alone. It seemed to want me to write it, but it wouldn't tell me how.

"Get Me a Kevin Costner Type"

I couldn't write the book, and I couldn't let the book go. So I decided to try actively not-writing it. The particular form of not-writing I happened onto for this project involved calling several of my characters into my office, one at a time, for a little chat. It was a bit like job interviews, a bit like sending down to central casting. One potential character talked himself out of a job. Another talked himself into a much bigger part. It was a revelation.

I thought I had invented this technique, but I have since heard from no less a writer than Elmore Leonard (twenty-eight novels and counting) that he "auditions" his characters. "They have to be able to talk," Leonard says. He has to "get their sound right," and he'll often drop one character in favor of another who turns out to be more interesting to him.

Here's a chunk of the conversation that took place in my head between my protagonist, a career minor-league manager named Dutch Brannigan, and the fictional character I became when I wrote myself into the dialogue.

"You going to ask me questions?"

"Or we can just talk."

Dutch doesn't look very comfortable with the notion of just talking. "You mind if I ask you a question first?" he says.

"Fire away."

"I was wondering," Dutch says, furrowing those marvelous eyebrows and hunching forward to lean over the table, "just how much of me is you. You know what I mean?"

"How much of my own personality will I put into you?"

"Yeah. Something like that."

"I don't know for sure. Probably quite a bit. There's some of me in each of you, but I think I feel closest to you."

Dutch nods. The cigar ash is about an inch long, and he starts to look around for a place to put it. I'm enjoying sucking in the good, rich second-hand smoke.

"That doesn't give you any particular privileges," I say.

"I don't get the last word, huh?"

"You don't even get to be right. Or at least, you don't get to be any righter than any of the others."

"Do you think of us as characters, or people, or what?"

"I want to think of you as people. I guess that's the main reason why I'm having these talks before we get the story going." . . .

I learned that Dutch reads a lot of baseball publications but no fiction, which embarrasses him, "You being a novelist and all," he says. I suggest he try W.P. Kinsella's *Shoeless Joe*.

"There's something I really want to ask you, Dutch," I say. "But I don't want to get too personal."

"That's kind of funny, if you think about it."

"I guess it is. Here goes, then. Do you still miss Molly?"

Dutch's face seems to soften, as if he's been clenching or holding himself in and has suddenly stopped. It's almost as if he's gone slightly out of focus. But he doesn't cry. If Dutch ever cries, it won't be in front of me.

"I miss her. Yes, I miss her very much." He thinks about that. "Except during the games. I don't think about her then. She was never a part of that."

The answer is so simple and so honest, I feel honored that he trusted me with it. . . .

"I'm not saying we didn't have our bad times," Dutch says. "And God knows, I was a long way from a perfect husband. A *long* way. But she . . . we shared so much."

"We're in trouble here, Dutch. You've got an emotion neither one of us has the words for."

Dutch smiles at that and nods again. He takes a long pull on the cigar. "You know what I miss most?" he says. "I miss the way she'd hum while she was working in the kitchen. Hummed all the time, mostly show tunes. And I miss the way the bathroom smelled when she got done fixing her face. That's what she called it, 'fixing her face.' And I miss sitting over a cup of coffee with her in the morning and reading the paper together, even if we didn't say a word. You miss the little everyday things."

"Careful. You'll have me stealing from McMurtry."

"Who?"

"Never mind. How's your boy?"

Dutch shrugs and breathes deeply through his nose. "You tell me," he says.

"I will if I can."

"I'd appreciate it. You know, or maybe you don't know, but Molly and me wanted to have five or six kids. When we found out we couldn't have another after Jimmy, it just about killed her. And then the way Jimmy put her through the jumps. . . ."

"That must have been pretty rough on you, too."

Dutch makes a soft growling noise deep in his throat. "I'm a hard-headed Irisher," he says. "I get by."

"You sure as hell do," I say.

"Is that it?"

"That's it. Thanks for coming in."

Dutch gets up. He's managed to get cigar ashes all over his tweed coat. He was born rumpled, I think.

"I don't suppose you can tell me how the season turns out," he says as I walk him to the door. "It's probably against the rules."

"I don't think there are any rules for what we're doing," I say. "But would you really want to know?"

"I suppose not," he says.

He's gone before it occurs to me that I'm not certain how the season will end.

The room stays full of cigar smoke after he leaves.

I may never use a line of this "interview" in the book. I've taken Dutch's cigars away from him and then given them back again, and changed his son's name to Tommy and discovered that his wife isn't really dead. Dutch has changed quite a bit in other ways as I've carried him through four chapters and a few fragments of chapters. And I'm sure he'll change considerably more before I'm done.

What I wrote, then, is in one sense a waste of time. But after I conducted this and several other conversations with my characters, I felt ready to begin writing at last. I learned more about my characters, and I also clarified for myself what I hoped to accomplish with the book. By developing a way to "not-write" my book, I had discovered a new channel for writing my way into it.

And I had also exercised my creativity by delving into my

shadow selves, aspects of my own personality that don't normally get expressed.

The Vigil of Silence

After making Eagle Scout, I had the honor of being invited to become a member of The Order of the Arrow. The initiation included a vigil, during which candidates were to remain silent for the two days of camp. I had probably never been silent for longer than two minutes, let alone two days, in my waking life, so the vigil of silence represented quite a challenge. I took the challenge seriously, met it and discovered that, with my outer voice stilled, I could hear a quieter, calmer inner voice. It was a good experience.

I'm not suggesting that you maintain a vigil of silence during your periods of creative procrastination, but I will suggest that you refrain from talking about your project with others.

In the idea-gathering stage, you should let everybody know what you're working on. They'll contribute material for the mental composting that helps you develop possibilities. But now, as the idea gets ready to take specific shape and form, you must protect it from the corrosive effect your words could have on it. Your imp wants to tell the story, remember, and does so strictly for the joy of the telling. If you let it blab the story now, the imp may lose all interest in telling it again, on paper, later.

"We did that one already," it may say when you summon it to the task.

"But that one didn't count," you'll protest—forgetting that imps never count. They only feel.

"But this one is for fame and fortune," you'll say—forgetting that imps don't care about fame and fortune. They only care about fun.

"Please," you'll beg, and your imp, a nice enough sort, after all, will say "Okay" and do its best.

But somehow its best just won't be as good as it could have been. The story won't be as textured, as detailed, because you've already told it, and some of the joy has gone out of it. Your first telling will likely be your best telling in terms of the richness of your invention. Save that first telling for putting words on paper.

Give Yourself a Deadline

If you've got somebody waiting for your writing, you have a powerful motive for writing it. That's one of the biggest benefits of a contract or assignment, of a writing class or critique group or even just a writing buddy with whom you swap manuscripts. If you've got a deadline, you've got a powerful motive for writing *now*.

The absence of deadlines can have a disastrous effect on the quality and quantity of writing you produce. A writer friend of mine, Ron Seely, produces marvelous feature articles on deadline for one of the daily newspapers here in town. He has written about Indian treaty rights, about adoption, about the homeless, all with precision, clarity and passion. He also handles news stories with skill and grace. He produces beautifully under pressure.

Last year this fine writer took a sabbatical from the paper, rented a cabin in the north woods of Wisconsin, and set out to write a novel. Every writer's dream, right? For my friend, it was a nightmare. He produced, in his words, "the worst novel ever written" and suffered considerably in the process. This fine deadline writer couldn't produce without pressure.

If you're writing on nobody's say-so but your own, you may need to set deadlines for yourself. If you can take forever to finish your project, that's how long it might take. Meanwhile, all the other wonderful ideas you could have entertained will get tired of waiting for your attention.

The more you get to know yourself as a writer, the better you'll get at setting reasonable deadlines. You want to push yourself a bit. "Before I die . . ." may not be a tight enough deadline to provide much motivation. But if you go too far in the other direction ("I'll have the first six chapters of my novel finished by Friday"), you'll set yourself up for failure and frustration. Set a deadline you can reach through hard work and application.

You'll be wise to break long projects into a series of small deadlines (not "I'll finish the book by April" but "I'll finish this chapter by Friday . . ."). Some writers work best with daily page or word quotas.

In deadline setting, as with all other aspects of creating an atmosphere for your creativity to flourish in, you must base your decisions on an honest and accurate appraisal of yourself as a writer. We all work differently. You must find *your* way.

10

Assembling the Tools
of the Trade

I moved from California to Wisconsin in 1979 with the intention of becoming a Real Writer—meaning a writer who gets words into print and (dare I even think it?) gets paid at least some money at least some of the time for those words.

I soon discovered that, to be a Real Writer, I needed a Real Writing Place. Before my projects got a home of their own, I was constantly picking up and setting down. I never had everything I needed when I needed it. I lost a lot of time, energy and momentum pitching my tent and then breaking camp again.

I carved out my RWP in a corner of the basement, behind the furnace, where I would bother no one, and no one would bother me. I got a second- (or third- or fourth-) hand metal desk from the Buy & Sell and a cast-off bookshelf from my wife's office. On the desk I centered my Olympia manual typewriter (which today stands next to the butter churn and the hand-crank telephone in the Museum of Ancient Stuff the Kids Don't Believe We Really Used). On the bookshelf I stacked my paper, ribbons and pencils, my envelopes and stamps, my reference books—a dictionary, my Strunk and White, a one-volume almanac, an atlas, a guide to old movies and television shows—and some of my best friends—Ken Kesey, William Faulkner, James Agee, William Stafford, Larry McMurtry.

That first summer, all the envelopes promptly sealed themselves, and the books swelled like sumo wrestlers.

"You need a dehumidifier," a neighbor told me.

In response to my blank stare, he added, "It's a box that sucks the water out of the air."

I didn't know about storm windows or driveway sealer, either. Californians lead sheltered lives.

That same neighbor would a few months later inform me that I also needed a humidifier, an attachment to the furnace to put water back *into* the air in winter.

Properly dehumidified in summer and humidified in winter, I settled in to write. I didn't listen to the ball game, sort the laundry, pay the bills, compute the taxes or clip newspaper articles in my real writing place. I only wrote.

In the summer my RWP was wondrously cool, in the winter downright cold. It was dark and dank at all times.

I spent a lot of time there. I even chained myself to the desk for an entire Labor Day weekend, writing a novel in seventy-two hours for a crazy contest sponsored by a Canadian publisher. I think I called the novel *The Boy Who Could See the Numbers*. It didn't win, but I learned just how wildly inventive the subconscious can become when pressed.

Gradually I added to the decor — some covers from *The New Yorker* for the bare concrete wall next to me; the seat cushion I bought at a Spokane Indians baseball game; my growing collection of the tubes they put newspapers in on rural routes; a Madison Muskies' line-up, in the manager's own hand, scored from the dugout by a friend on my birthday; a poster of Beany and Cecil the Seasick Sea Serpent, donated by my mother-in-law; my collection of baseball caps.

A poor place, perhaps, but distinctly mine own.

At times I dreamed of loftier quarters — fireplace, skylight, oak bookshelves, views of the forest or the seashore. But I didn't spend much time dreaming. Mostly I spent my writing time writing. Eventually I had thirty stories, articles and queries in the mail. When one came back wounded, I patched it up as best I could and sent it back into battle the next morning. When I got three rejections in one day, as happened on two or three occasions, I consoled myself with the knowledge that I still had twenty-seven live ones in the air or on editors' desks.

Gradually the acceptances began to punctuate the rejections and give me reason and will to keep on writing.

I never missed an appointment to be in my RWP. If an idea happened to swim by, I was ready to try to net it. If inspiration didn't appear, I wrote anyway.

I've since graduated to a downtown office with a lake view. Instead of that old manual Olympic, I compose on a Macintosh SE/30 now. My tools are fancier, but I still surround myself with silly things that make me happy — my *Baseball America* calendar of minor league ballparks, my George Bush dog chew toy, a model dinosaur (brontosaurus, I think) with a miniature Los Angeles Dodgers batting helmet perched on its head, my Batman bank, a picture of wife, son and dog at Mirror Lake, my ever-expanding collections of baseball caps and newspaper tubes.

I've still got my references within arm's reach, along with some new friends on the shelves. (The males-only club has been crashed by folks like Dorothea Brande, Natalie Goldberg and Brenda Ueland. You'll hear more about them in a minute.)

And I still keep all my writing appointments.

It doesn't matter so much what the place looks like, what you write with or on, what talismans you keep nearby, which friends populate your bookshelves. Only these things matter:

1. You need a place where you only write.
2. You need to have your tools close at hand.
3. You need to keep your writing appointments.

No stalling. No self-induced distractions. No long start-up and break-down time. No chatter about "writer's block" or "feeling inspired." Just you and the keyboard (or pen or pencil or whatever).

Develop a strict discipline regarding time and place for your writing and you will impose a measure of discipline on your free-spirited muse, you will affirm and encourage her with your attention and time, and you will give her a familiar, comfortable atmosphere to create in.

However, that doesn't mean that you should limit your writing to your writing place or that you should ever feel dependent on that combination of place and tools to inspire you. Like Dumbo's magic feather, your RWP can give you confidence and focus your energies, but the feather doesn't make you fly. Your muse takes care of that, and she can do it without any special runways for taking off and landing if she has to.

Magic Word Machine — Good Slave But Lousy Master

For years I used hand clippers to trim the hedges and bushes. It was hot, sweaty work, and it took a couple of days to finish the job.

Then one summer my wife bought me an electric hedge trimmer. I was skeptical at first (and even a bit scared I might lop off a few fingers). But after some initial awkward thrusts and a few mangled bushes, I learned to handle my new tool. Now I finish the job in hours instead of days, leaving me more time for writing and for all the not-writing things I want and need to do. And I do a much better job on the hedges and bushes.

I found the word processor to be even more intimidating than the hedge trimmer, but the transition has been even more gratifying.

When my boss at the University bought me my first magic word machine, a Compaq, several years ago, I left it in its crate for six weeks. You weren't going to get me up in one of those things. No way. If God had intended for us to use computers, we would have been born with floppy discs as standard issue.

But I watched one of my colleagues, Blake Kellogg, get up and running on his computer. After a lot of initial swearing and head-banging, he seemed to be enjoying himself thoroughly. He also talked about increased productivity and better work. I remembered how hard the transition from writing in longhand to creating on the keyboard had been. The pain had paid big dividends in increased productivity, greater willingness to revise, and thus, better writing.

I realized, too, that I'd had a tough time going from a manual to an electric typewriter. I thought I'd never get used to the darn thing humming at me all the time. Whenever I'd stop to think, it seemed to be saying, "What's the matter, hmmmmmmmm?" But I had made that adjustment, too, and the payoff in increased productivity, while not as dramatic as the gains I made with my initiation to composing on the keyboard, were enough to make the initial discomfort worth enduring.

So maybe, just maybe, I reasoned, it might be worth the effort to master the computer, for all its alien beeps and blips and blinking lights.

By the time I was finally ready to give it a go, Blake had mastered the program and was kind enough to help me up the learning curve. After two hours of losing copy into the ether and locking myself out of programs, I was hooked. Man and machine had bonded. I knew I'd never go back.

It hasn't always been easy. No marriage of opposites is. I once lost over three hour's worth of first draft when the plug on the computer came loose. (As I type this, I remember to save into memory everything I've written this session.) Each new program has meant new learning and new frustrations.

But the magic box has made me a better writer, and I think I know why. Creativity involves taking risks, after all. You have to take chances, try things out, discover your material and your approach as you go. A good word-processing program, with its "delete," "cut and paste" and "spell check" and the rest, removes the penalty for failure. If you don't like the words you've created, you can easily move them, change them or chuck them. After awhile, you come to understand at last that, in the initial stages of writing, there are no mistakes, only possibilities.

I've become bilingual, with an IBM at home and a Macintosh at work. The DOS-based IBM works with words and numbers; Mac uses pictures. I prefer the Mac, because I tend to think in pictures, but my wife likes the IBM best. It really doesn't matter, especially now that software programs like "windows" enable a DOS system to work pretty much like a Mac. Whatever program and computer you use, they can help to liberate your creativity.

But you must remain the master of, not the slave to, the new technology. You're no more obligated to learn every aspect of every program than you are to cook every dish in a cookbook. And you don't have to know how the box does its magic, any more than you need to know how an internal combustion engine works in order to drive a car. You only need to know what you need to know to do your work.

If you branch out into other areas later, as I did when I began exploring print design for my self-published book and my newsletters for writers, your experience with word processing will help you master new programs or new aspects of old programs.

As much as I love my computers and wouldn't think of going back to longhand or even the typewriter, I know that my creativity isn't dependent on fancy tools or toys, just as it isn't bound to particular time and place. No matter what tools you master as you practice the writing trade, never lose your ability to create with blunt Crayola on paper sack while riding the bus to work. Your muse will continue to surprise and delight you at odd times and in strange places, presenting you with ideas, images, whole chunks of creation. Always be ready and willing to accept those gifts.

Take a Few Friends Along for Company

Most of us write alone. You may hum or whisper, mumble or mutter, scream or laugh. You probably read your stuff aloud at some stage in the process. But you get only empty echoes in response. No one applauds when you type "The End" to a project. It's a lonely business.

Rejection is cold and silent. So is acceptance. Often the finished words don't appear in print until months or even years after you've written them, and when they do, the world seems to take scant notice.

So I always take a few friends along with me for company when I write. They have to be quiet while I'm working, of course, have to wait until and unless I call on them for help. But when I need them, they're always there for me.

I call on my paperback *Oxford American Dictionary* more than all my other friends combined. Any good, unabridged dictionary will do, and my choice was arbitrary, I'm sure. But this one seldom lets me down. For me it's where the words live.

I don't use a thesaurus, although I know many writers who do. The thesaurus is a good resource when you have the general idea but not the precise word. But it can be the devil's tool. If you have a perfectly acceptable word, like "fire," but crave something fancier, the thesaurus will tempt you to use "conflagration." So I stick to the dictionary, which for me is less likely to be a temptation to stray from plain style.

I also refer to the *Associated Press Stylebook*, which arbitrates silly domestic quarrels such as how to signify "in the morning." (Is it "AM," or "A.M." or "a.m."? — certainly not "am," "Am" or "aM.") I don't want to spend a lot of time fussing over such mundane matters, but I also want to use a style that's acceptable to editors and readers and that won't call attention to itself. That's why I use AP style. There are several other good style books available, but most publications use AP or a close variant. (According to AP, it's "a.m.," by the way).

I've read dozens of books on grammar and usage, but the champ for me is still the one I met in freshmen composition many years ago — *The Elements of Style*, by William Strunk and E.B. White (Macmillan). You can read it in a couple of sittings, and you'll refer to it for the rest of your life. It's the grammar book for adults — sophisticated, elevated and elevating. None of this business of underlining the subject once and the predicate twice and then turning the page to see if you did it right.

I also like Rene Cappon's *Associated Press Guide to Good News Writing*, a marvelous discussion of ways to achieve precision and clarity in writing. Don't let the title fool you; it's good for all types of writing. You can order it directly from the AP in New York City. If you come across a book by Cappon called *The Word*, grab it. Same book before they changed the title.

You learn to write by writing, of course, and by reading the work of your chosen mentors. But you can learn a lot about writing by reading about writing, too, as long as you don't let the reading become a substitute for the writing.

I'll pick up and read anything by William L. Rivers, a marvelous writer on writing. Ditto William Zinsser, whose *On Writing Well* (Harper & Row) remains a classic and contains the best chapter on sports writing I've encountered. He also has a wonderful book on the trials and triumphs of learning how to use the word processor.

I found John Gardner's *On Becoming a Novelist* (Tarcher) inspirational as well as informative and imagine it would be helpful and nurturing even if you weren't attempting a novel.

Ray Bradbury's *Zen in the Art of Writing* (Capra Press) is a marvelous exposition of the creative process in writing. Bradbury describes a process he has used successfully for fifty years of original writing.

Chuck Amuck: The Life and Times of an Animated Cartoonist (Avon Books) wouldn't seem to belong on a writer's bookshelf. But Chuck Jones, creator of the Road Runner and Wile E. Coyote and midwife to Bugs Bunny, Daffy Duck and scores of other cartoon characters, writes with humor and insight on the creative process. I treasure this book.

The good folks at Writer's Digest, who brought you this book, have provided some wonderful references, including Lawrence Block's *Writing the Novel: From Plot to Print* and Gary Provost's *Make Your Words Work*. WD's books on specific genres are the best I've seen anywhere.

Block's *Write for Your Life* is a guide to help you talk back to those squelchers we discussed earlier. Block self-published the book to back-up his seminar by the same name, but the book is out of print and might be hard to find.

For a general jumpstart to get the creative juices going, I like

Roger Von Oech's *A Whack on the Side of the Head* (Warner).

And for refreshment and help in really paying attention to my surroundings, I revisit *The Zen of Seeing* (Vintage), Frederick Franck's guide to seeing and drawing as meditation.

I mentioned earlier in this chapter that I had finally integrated my all-male writer's club. That started a few years back with Dorothea Brande's *Becoming a Writer*. Some folks thought they invented meditation and visualization in the 1960s. Brande knew all about it, and was applying it to the writing process, in the 1930s. Tarcher reissued her wonderful book in the early 1980s.

I've since discovered two more women (don't know what took me so long) who deserve space on the top shelf with Brande. Brenda Ueland's *If You Want to Write* (Graywolf) is a manifesto, a declaration of independence, a liberation of the writer's spirit. And Natalie Goldberg's *Writing Down the Bones* (Shambhala) is as wise as it is exciting in exploring why as well as how we write. Goldberg has a new book out (new as I write this, anyway) called *Wild Mind: Living the Writer's Life* (Bantam – New Age). I didn't find the sequel quite as exciting as the first book (perhaps because it isn't as good a book, perhaps simply because the element of surprise was gone) but can recommend it as well.

If you want some help with business writing, try Deborah Dumaine's *Write to the Top: Writing for Corporate Success* (Random House).

And if you're thinking of attempting a self-publishing project, don't do it until you read *Is There a Book Inside You?* by Dan Poynter and Mindy Bingham (Poynter's own Para Publishing, and a Writer's Digest Book Club Main Selection).

For a fine discussion of the world of book publishing, try John Boswell's *The Awful Truth About Publishing* (Warner).

These books have helped me to become a better writer and to take greater pleasure in being the writer I've become. I think they can help you, too.

Then there's room on my shelf for my mentors. Their books don't speak directly about the writer's craft. They embody it. We each have to find our own favorites, the writings that nurture us. Among my favorites are James Agee's *A Death in the Family*, William Faulkner's *Light in August*, Ernest Hemingway's *The Old Man and the Sea*, W.P. Kinsella's *Shoeless Joe*, William Saroyan's *The Human Comedy*, Ken Kesey's *Sometimes a Great Notion* and Larry McMurtry's

Lonesome Dove—perennial refreshment and perennial challenge. I have several books by Wallace Stegner, who taught me in college, and dozens of volumes of short stories. I especially enjoy Flannery O'Connor and Carson McCullers, whom I got attached to as a college freshman.

Pick your friends carefully. They will teach, nurture and sustain you. They will alter the way you look at the world as well as the way you write about it.

Don't wait until you have all your tools assembled before you start to write. Write now, while beginning or continuing to accumulate your friends, mentors and guides.

11

Previewing Coming Attractions

"I don't outline anymore," best-selling novelist Elmore Leonard recently told a writers conference in Madison. "I used to, but it took all the fun out of it."

Leonard, author of twenty-eight westerns and crime novels, likes to discover his plots as he goes along. He always knows when he's getting near the end of a book, he says, but "I don't know how it's going to end. I don't want to know."

Not-outlining works for Leonard. He doesn't want an outline to limit the creative possibilities. And not-outlining probably works for you sometimes, too. When you know what you want to say and you feel ready to say it, or when you're willing to give the muse free reign to roam, don't hold yourself up playing outline games.

But what about those times when you need to know where you're going in order to know what direction to start out in? And what do you do when you don't know how to begin? You've got thoughts and images strewn all over your mental floor, but your ideas just refuse to line up and march in formation.

Give an Outline a Chance

For those times, an outline may help a lot. If the very word "outline" gives you the shivers and shudders, I'll bet you learned to outline the same way I did. (See the example at right.)

When I first started teaching English composition, I made my students create these kinds of documents. A particularly honest, brave and/or foolhardy student came to my office one day for help with his outlining and, in a fit of frustration, admitted that he usually

I. Use Roman numerals for main ideas.
  A. Indent five spaces for secondary ideas.
  B. Use capital letters for secondary ideas.
    i. Use lowercase Romans for tertiary ideas.
    ii. Indent five more spaces for tertiary ideas.
II. Parallel statements must be expressed in parallel form.
Oops.
II. Express parallel statements in parallel form.
  And so on, until you and the subject are exhausted.

just wrote the essay first and then wrote the outline. I started to get self-righteous, but then I remembered that I'd done the same thing as a student. You, too? After all, it's a whole lot easier that way. You can't really create this kind of outline until you know exactly what you want to say, in the order you want to say it.

I soon stopped requiring formal outlines. The Roman numeral/ parallel structure format is just no help in getting your thoughts organized, which is precisely what an outline is supposed to do.

So let's throw the formal outline out and see if we can discover a more flexible outlining format that will help. I'll offer six ways to get organized. I've used each at one time or another, depending on the project and my degree of confusion. I hope you'll find one or more methods that work for you.

You can use these techniques before you've done any research, as a way of taking mental inventory and discovering what you know and how you feel about a topic. And you can use them again after you've gathered all your information, as an informal way of organizing your thoughts before your write.

1. Bubble Outlining

The Roman numeral outline is linear, orderly and sequential, which makes it just right for analyzing other people's work. But by imposing its rigid order on the material, a linear outline closes out the possibility of generating new combinations of ideas. You may want to try an outlining technique that is circular instead of linear and that relies on free association rather than correct answers and chronological certainty.

Try a bubble outline (a.k.a. "circular map," "spoke outline," "tree outline" and "tornado outline"). Instead of starting in the upper left-hand corner of the page with Roman numeral I, start in the middle of a large sheet of paper (make sure to give yourself plenty of room for this rather messy project) and write down the idea you want to write about.

For purposes of demonstration, I'll use this chapter as an example. In the center of the page for my bubble outline on chapter eleven, "Previewing," I might write, "How to organize your thoughts before your write."

Draw an oval (or bubble) around your main idea. Then write down all the ideas you can think of that relate to the topic. It doesn't matter where or in what order you put the ideas on the page. Just write them down as they occur to you, wherever they seem to fit best. You don't have to use complete sentences or even coherent phrases. You can use key words, symbols, cartoons, anything, as long as you know what you mean. (Remember, this is a working paper, for your eyes only.)

For this chapter, I wrote in random bunches around the central idea: bubble outline, Leonard, free association, brave student, Roman numerals, interviewing/auditioning, brick-laying, one-per-card, computer doodling, visualization, file folders.

When you think you're finished, wait a few moments, pencil in hand, to see what else might come.

Then draw ovals around each thought and begin to look for connections. Draw lines to link related ideas. Jot in quote, image or anecdote fragments and statistics around the relevant ideas.

With your material laid out before you, you're able to discover your organization. You're allowing your mind to free associate and thus create new connections, new categories, new information from the melding of existing words and images.

No English teacher could love such a chaotic, idiosyncratic mess, but it will help you get ready to write.

Cross out irrelevant entries. Search for gaps. Now's the time to go get the information you need.

When you're ready, put a "1" by the idea you think you want to start with, a "2" by the next main idea, and so on until you've run out of ideas. Notice how the organization begins to take shape as you work. The bubble outline is organic and malleable. All judgments are tentative. You can always scratch out a number and assign a new place to an idea.

By the time you finish your bubble outline, you'll have explored, developed and organized your material.

2. Brick-laying

As flexible as the bubble outline is, it still requires that you put your ideas on a piece of paper in some sort of relationship to one another. If you're not ready for even that much commitment to a particular shape and form, or if your idea is too involved and complicated to fit on even a large sheet of butcher paper, get yourself a pack of notecards instead.

Write one idea, image, quote, anecdote or statistic per notecard. Write the ideas as they occur to you. You'll discover and impose the order later. Give yourself a little time with the cards even after you're pretty sure you're done, so you can be sure to collect the straggler ideas.

Now spread your cards out on a large, flat surface. Move related ideas close together. Slide examples under the ideas they support. Begin stacking related ideas. (To me this part seems a little like making a wall out of bricks, which is why I call the process "brick-laying." I suppose you could just as well call it "crazy eights" or "table tennis.")

Throw out irrelevant cards and seek out information to fill the gaps.

You'll wind up with a deck of cards approximating the organization of the piece you want to write. If you change your mind, you can rearrange the cards. You can also shuffle them, throw them against the wall or toss them out the window. Brick-laying is an extremely flexible form of outlining.

Now you're ready to deal yourself a winning piece of writing.

3. The Cafeteria Plate Outline

My parents used to take my brother and me to Lake Arrowhead, high up in the San Bernardino Mountains of Southern California, for our summer vacations. The years have tempered my memories of car sickness, boredom and backseat boxing matches. But I vividly remember the lake, with its swimming and fishing, and the Swiss-style village that offered miniature golf, movies and an arcade (pre-video variety — we're talking ski-ball).

And I remember, too, the village cafeteria and its plastic plates. My colleague, Blake, has since taught me how much you can learn about organization from the lowly cafeteria plate. The big compartment was for the meat loaf, the medium compartment was for the mashed potatoes and gravy, and the little compartment was for the peas. Meat loaf never went in the mashed potatoes compartment, and peas never wandered into the gravy (unless, of course, you wanted to slop them all together in willful disregard for order). Dessert got its own plate (but only if you finished your peas).

It worked for meat loaf, mashed potatoes and peas, and it works for long, complicated writing projects.

For example, I used a combination of bubble mapping, bricklaying and just plain scribbling to divide the information for this book into fourteen chapters. That's much too much to try to organize in detail using the techniques we've discussed so far. So I got fourteen file folders, one for each chapter. On the cover of each folder, I put the name of the chapter and a rough outline of what was to go into it. Every time I came across a good quote or anecdote, and every time I had an idea I thought might work for that chapter, I stuck the scribbled note, newspaper clip or whatever into the folder.

As I created the rough drafts for my chapters, I put them into the appropriate folders, too, so that I could keep revising, reworking and adding as the book grew.

That way none of the chapter four stuff (meat loaf) got into the chapter five folder (peas). And I had plenty of room inside the meat loaf chapter to add more oats.

The folders went wherever I went, and they allowed me a great deal of freedom to move material around. Each chapter remained open to new possibilities even after I'd written the rough draft.

4. Outlining by Design

Walk into any print designer's studio, and you're liable to see a series of pieces of paper taped to the walls. These are sketches of the pages or panels of the project the designer is working on.

Designers use the wall as a way of gaining perspective. What ideas dominate? Do the pages or panels look graphically related, even at a distance? Does the material flow, not just within a given article, but within a sixty-four page magazine? Does the organization make visual as well as contextual sense?

It's a way of being sure you don't lose the forest for the trees.

The same sort of perspective can be useful for you as a writer. Tack your ideas to a wall or bulletin board and step back. See your writing project as a unified, harmonious whole rather than a series of chunks.

William Faulkner apparently used this off-the-wall technique to help himself keep track of the amazingly complex, multi-generational fictional world he created out of the real world of Oxford, Mississippi. It worked for Faulkner, and it can work for you.

5. Computer Doodling

If you use word processing, you may have already stumbled onto this technique, a combination of notetaking, outlining and rough drafting. I use it in my magazine article work, but I'm sure you can modify it for other types of writing as well.

I take key word and phrase interview notes and then go back over my notes as soon after the interview as possible, so I can recall the exact words my subject used and the inflections of those words. I transcribe these notes directly into the computer.

I used to print out a copy of all my notes for an article, let them simmer for a few days, and mark them up with a felt-tip pen, looking for slants, leads and closers. I'd also create some sort of an outline if I was having trouble getting started.

Leave it to a lazy man to find an easier way. With deadlines pressing me, I began cutting corners. Instead of making a complete copy of my notes, I began pulling out main ideas and key quotes. Instead of writing notes, I found myself writing copy, which is to say that what I wrote sounded more like an article and less like notes to myself.

I began growing whole paragraphs that way. Then I'd use the "cut and paste" options in my word processing program to rearrange paragraphs until I had a rough approximation of the final article — emphasis on the rough. Seams showed, loose ends dangled, quotes meandered. But still, I was a couple of large steps ahead of myself, going directly from notes in a notebook to rough, rough draft on the computer screen. Even a rough, rough draft is a lot better than a pile of notes.

I don't think I could have tried this technique when I first started writing articles, and it doesn't always work for me now, even after ten years of fairly steady output. But when this technique works, it saves a great deal of time.

6. Roman Numerals Without the Roman Numerals

If you're uncomfortable with all this unorthodox outlining, you may want to go back to something closer to linear outlining you learned in school. But now that no teacher is waiting with red pen in one hand and grade book in the other, let's lighten up and see if we can get the thing to work for instead of against you.

Forget the Roman numerals. Forget the parallel structure. Just jot down your ideas, indenting for less important ideas and supporting details.

If you're working on a computer, it's quite simple to move ideas around until you get them in an order that seems to work. If you're using pencil and paper, you can get the same effect with scissors and tape. If your mind tends to run in a fairly orderly, linear fashion, then help it to run that way.

Combine and modify methods. Use different methods on different projects. Develop a system or systems that work for you. Be flexible in your approach.

But whatever way you organize your materials, approach the project creatively, which is to say, be as open to possibilities as you can be, for as long as you can be.

12

Keeping That Writing Appointment

In chapter nine, I advised you to make a writing appointment and then let your project simmer in your subconscious for a day or two.

Now it's time to keep that appointment.

Keeping your writing appointment is probably the most important trait you can develop. Creativity involves being open to your insights and nurturing your inspirations, but it also involves the discipline of sitting down to write regularly, in sickness and in health, in good times and in bad, inspired or not.

Fight the urge to quit, to excuse yourself, to put it off. Keep that appointment, and the next one, and the one after that. Don't waste any energy deciding whether or not you're going to write. That shouldn't even be an issue. Direct all your energy to the images and ideas you want to create on paper.

But what about those times when the words and images just don't want to emerge? We all come to the writing reluctantly sometimes. For those times, maybe all you need is a good warm-up.

Stretching Out the Muscles and Warming Up the Will

It's the most dramatic moment in baseball. Bottom of the ninth, game on the line, starting pitcher faltering. In from the bullpen strides the ace relief pitcher. Some walk *slowly*; some trot. Some glower at the opposition; some talk to the baseball. All have techniques for mastering the tension, focusing their concentration and harnessing the energy needed to get the job done.

Now back up a few minutes and watch that relief pitcher as he gets up to throw in the bullpen before entering the game. At first he throws softly, from well in front of the mound, just stretching out his muscles. Then he steps back onto the mound and begins to throw harder, first fastballs, which take less out of the arm, and finally breaking pitches.

He's getting his body ready, protecting himself from injury and making sure that his first pitch in a game situation will be effective. He's also getting his mind ready, going over the hitters and how he plans to get them out. And he's probably getting his spirit ready as well, focusing his energy and visualizing himself performing effectively.

The routine varies with the sport, of course, but all athletes warm-up before entering the competition.

Writers run less of a risk of pulling a hamstring muscle or throwing a wild pitch if they neglect their warm-ups. But a little stretching of the creative muscles can help you start strong and perform creatively throughout your writing session.

Here are a few of my favorite warm-ups. You'll probably want to add some of your own and modify these to suit your needs.

1. Directed Flow-writing

You can use a modification of the don't stop/don't think/don't lie method you will be using in the 21-Day Miracle Writing Plan (pages 145 and 146), as a way of warming up for your writing session. Put your subject at the top of the page or computer screen and simply write whatever comes to mind for ten or fifteen minutes of nonstop free association. Don't analyze or evaluate what you write. Don't worry about whether or not you'll be able to use any of it later. This isn't about "using." Just write.

Flow-writing helps to get you warmed up, and it also allows you to recognize and express your feelings about your topic. You may discover a strong bias or emotional reaction you weren't even aware of. Knowing about such feelings will make you a better writer because, if left unexpressed, those feelings might create mental disharmony and distract you while you write.

The transition from warm-up to writing may be effortless; flow-writing may merge naturally into the actual story or article or chapter you're writing. But even if your warm-up doesn't go quite that smoothly, directed flow-writing will get you primed and ready to write. By the time you've been writing steadily and comfortably for ten or fifteen minutes, it's way too late to even consider getting writer's block.

2. Sit Right Down and Write Yourself a Letter

You may not be ready to write to a reader. But you're probably ready to write to yourself.

Compose a "Dear me" letter, telling yourself exactly what you intend to write about, what points you'll stress, what impact you'd like to have on the reader. Relax and have a good chat with yourself. Don't worry about organization, grammar or syntax. You're writing to someone who knows and understands you well and will forgive your misspellings.

You could have this internal chat in your head, of course. And doing so would help you to get organized and focused for the day's work. But part of the idea here is to get the fingers moving and the words forming on paper, so go ahead and write it down.

You can address your letter to a good friend or even to the editor who'll eventually be reading the finished product if that helps you get started. The key is that you relax and write comfortably and unself-consciously. As with flow-writing, you'll get the words flowing naturally and also focus yourself on the project at hand.

3. Let Your Character Write to You

Get inside the head of one of your characters by writing a letter to yourself from that character's point of view.

This method works for fiction or nonfiction, the major difference being that in fiction you're making up the unique consciousness struggling to express itself in words, while in nonfiction you're using the information you gathered in interviews and other research to create thoughts as you would imagine your subject would have and express them. Either way, you're getting to know your character and your intentions while you're warming up.

4. Disparate Elements: Pictures

Creativity often involves the joining of two previously unrelated ideas. You can get yourself thinking creatively by artificially inducing a few such couplings.

Cut interesting pictures out of magazines and keep them in your writing place. The more ambiguous the picture, the better it will work. Cut off the captions; you won't want any hints as to what the picture is supposed to represent.

For a writing warm-up, pluck three or four pictures at random from the pile and spend ten minutes trying to make a story out of them.

For one of my writing warm-ups, I selected a picture of a man wading through a flooded living room. The water was chin high, so that his head appeared to be bobbing along by itself. Next I pulled out a picture of a rather heavyset young man, beer can in hand, leer on face, leaning back on the seat of a "Harley hog" motorcycle. My third picture was of a high-wire walker, using a long pole to keep his balance while the camera caught him from below.

What would you make of these images? Why not take a minute to find out?

I spent a few minutes playing with the images, which merged with a news story I had just read about the three hundred thousand bikers who had converged on the tiny town of Sturgis, South Dakota, in the fabled Black Hills. I concocted a little tale about the flood that hit Sturgis during the biker's convention and the heroic biker who managed to go for help by walking a wire across the flooded valley.

You won't win a Pulitzer writing this sort of stuff, but that's not the point. You're simply getting the juices flowing and taking the sting out of those first few lonely moments with the computer, typewriter or pad of paper.

My writer friend Shiela Reaves uses a wonderful variation on this technique when she's trying to think of effective images. (She's also a photographer, so she's always thinking in terms of image.) For example, she once faced the challenge of coming up with an image for a magazine cover designed to illustrate the high cost of weddings. She made two lists—one of symbols for high cost, the second for symbols for weddings. If you like, take a few minutes and come up with your own lists before reading on.

My first list includes a huge dollar sign, greenbacks with wings, an ever-escalating bar graph, a man with his pockets turned out to indicate his penniless state, a checkbook strapped to a rocket ship and so on.

The second list includes church, altar, rings, showers of rice, multi-tiered cake with miniature bride and groom on top. . . . Again, you could probably come up with a long list.

Most of these images are pretty trite. But watch what happens when you combine an image from the money list with an image from the wedding list, to create a fresh image that embodies the high cost of weddings. Give it a try if you like.

Shiela took the little bride and groom on the wedding cake and turned the groom's pockets inside out to create her image. She arranged a marriage of meanings by fixing up two strangers for a blind date that worked out.

5. Disparate Elements: Words

You can use words as well as images to play this game. Every time you come across an interesting noun, jot it on a notecard, one noun per card. Keep the card collection handy. When you're ready to warm up, draw out four or five cards and write a paragraph that incorporates all the words.

For example, for one writing warm-up I drew the following words: banana, rock, Dalmatian, beach, Tesla, (Sure, I toss proper names into the mix, too. I heard about Tesla on a Wisconsin Public Radio talk show. He was a scientist/engineer who never got credit for his inventions, one of which, according to the fellow on the radio, was the radio itself.)

What would you make of these five words?

I like to see if I can use the words in an unusual or unexpected way. So for this exercise, I got an image of the great inventor Tesla taking a vacation at the beach, where he trained his pet Dalmatian to bring him a banana daiquiri on the rocks.

Again, no Pulitzer Prizes here, just a mental unlimbering to ready me for the task at hand.

6. Disparate Elements: Concepts

Imagine a room full of high-powered business executives. They've paid a lot of money to fly in a consultant to help them come up with solutions to some marketing problems that have had them stuck for months. The consultant eyes them solemnly.

"I'm going to ask you a question," he tells them. "I want you to come up with as many answers to the question as you can in the next five minutes."

He turns to the flip chart and writes "banana" and "bell." For the next five minutes," he says, "you are to come up with a list of as many ways as you can think of that a banana is different than a bell."

Before they can protest, the consultant shouts "Go" and walks out of the room.

Unlikely? Actually, scenes just like this are going on in corporate meeting rooms all over the country as executives discover the value of disparate thinking. By creating collisions of ideas in the mind, they are able to come up with innovative ways of looking at their problems and their customers' needs. If you've ever bought potato chips in one of those tubes that looks like it ought to hold tennis balls, you've enjoyed the results of this kind of brainstorming session.

Try it out. Just how is a banana different than a bell? Write down as many ways as you can think of in one minute before reading on.

Here's what I came up with:

- You can eat a banana, but you can't (or at least probably shouldn't) eat a bell.
- Bananas are yellow (or, if you wait long enough, black). Bells are, well, bell-colored.
- Bananas rot. Bells don't.
- Bananas are soft. Bells are hard.
- Bananas have peels. Bells don't.
- Banana peels split into sections. Bells don't (although the Liberty Bell has a crack).
- Nobody goes to Philadelphia to see the Liberty Banana.

Now it gets a little tougher — and more fun. Next question: "How is a banana *like* a bell?"

Want to play along for a minute before reading on?

Here are my profound reflections on banana and bellness:

- Bananas have peels, and bells peal.
- Actually, bells *do* rot. It just takes longer.
- Sure, nobody goes all the way to Philadelphia to see a banana, but a lot of folks like bananas, and some folks go bananas over bells.
- A banana can serve as a symbol (male virility), just as the Liberty Bell serves as a symbol (freedom).

Our high-priced business consultant would now make those executives go one important step further by asking, "How could you design a better bell by making it more like a banana?

This works only if the executives allow themselves to have silly, seemingly unworkable ideas, such as an edible bell or a bell with a peel (along with a peal and appeal).

You can focus this kind of word and idea play on a specific problem in your writing ("How is my hero like a bicycle?"), or you can simply pick two subjects at random from your box of noun cards, as a way to get yourself into a playful, non-judgmental and thus creative frame of mind.

7. Random Influence

Some folks believe that the way their tea leaves congregate in the bottom of the cup or the way the Tarot cards fall can predict their future. Some look for guidance from the alignment of the stars (astrology) or from the number of letters in their names (numerology). Others open the Bible and select a passage at random, believing that the passage will have special significance for them.

How about you? Can you see the future reflected in the seemingly random patterns of coffee grounds or dandruff?

At the heart of such belief is the notion that the events in question aren't really random at all, that an unseen force guides the fall of the cards or the selection of the Bible passage, that the hand on the deck of cards somehow influences their order.

Whether or not you believe in these or other ways of discerning meaning and order in the universe, you can use a random outside influence to spark your creativity and help you to warm up for your writing session.

Pick up the morning newspaper and select a word or phrase at random. For example, you might decide to take the fifth word of the fifth line of the fifth column of the fifth page. I just tried it with the August 16, 1990 issue of the Montpelier, Vermont *Times Argus* and came up with . . . a three column market ad. So I changed all the fives to sixes and got . . . another blank, because page six, the editorial page, has only five columns. So I simply pointed to a word at random and got "education." Reading the whole phrase yielded "essential early education programs."

I could then write a five-minute warm-up on "essential early education programs." I could be serious ("Headstart programs have had a positive impact on our society and should be funded at an increasing level despite the need to eliminate the budget deficit") or silly ("Every child should learn how to spit, whistle and yodel and should be tested on these essential skills before being allowed to enter the first grade.") Either way, I would know absolutely nothing about what I was talking about, but I'd have a good warm-up.

I could also try to apply the phrase to the task at hand. How might "essential early education" apply to a book on writing creatively, for example? Can kids be taught to be creative? Or is it more a matter of not crushing their natural creativity? If creativity is innate and natural, how come we lose touch with it as we get older and more educated? How might reflection on this topic help me to get in touch with my own creativity?

Such reflections might lead to something useful. They might spark questions or tangents that will yield dividends later. They might help you to see your subject from a new angle. Or they might be a totally silly diversion—but nevertheless a wonderful way to get warmed up and writing without the whole process having to be painful.

You can find other sources of words, phrases or images, of course. Since the influence is random, by definition it doesn't much matter where it comes from.

And the list doesn't have to be random. Ray Bradbury got started as a writer by developing a list of words that had personal meaning for him. He then started a writing session by taking a word/memory and writing about it. He developed some of his best stories this way, using a word as a key to unlock stored memory.

8. Visualization

We now have word processors to help us with our work, but we are the true word processors. We read words, we listen to them, we speak them, we think with them and, of course, we try to get them to dance on the page to the rhythms we devise for them.

From time to time, all that word processing can make us word-bound. Visualization is a fine writer's warm-up and a wonderful way to escape words for a bit.

Instead of trying to think of the words, create pictures of the project you're tackling. For example, let's suppose you're writing a story or article (this works equally well for fiction or nonfiction) centered on a maverick trial attorney named Jack McManus. (I happen to be working on such a profile at the moment.) Instead of trying to develop a word description of McManus, I'll create a mental picture of him. I'll make that picture as detailed as possible — shape and size, posture, color of hair and eyes, distinguishing features, clothes, the western art in his office.

When the still life is fairly vivid, set it into motion. I'll picture the way Jack leans forward to emphasize a point and the way he walks with a slight hitch, souvenir of an airplane crash some years ago. For a fictional character, make up those little everyday scenes that may never make it into the story. See your protagonist digging into her Wheaties with sliced bananas (or leftover lemon meringue pie or whatever you think she eats for breakfast). Imagine her driving to work. Is she a considerate driver, or does she become a demon behind the wheel?

Now put another character in front of her and let her react. Note how she stands while listening. Hear her speech patterns. What does her face look like when she's angry but doesn't want to show it?

When you've watched her for a few minutes, write down what you saw. After ten minutes of writing, you'll know your character a lot better, and you'll be warmed up and ready to write.

How Other Creative People Have Goosed the Muse

Do you use caffeine to give yourself a jumpstart? If so, you're in good company. Balzac drank more than fifty cups of coffee a day and poured out a torrent of books, publishing eight in 1842 alone. He brewed his coffee in the Turkish fashion, creating a thick caffeine mush that caused ideas, in his words "to pour out like regiments of the Grand Army over the battlefield." Balzac won many battles but lost the war. He died of caffeine poisoning.

William Faulkner said the only tools a writer really needs are paper, tobacco, food and whiskey.

Tom Batiuk, creator of the "Funky Winkerbean" cartoon strip, says he relies on a different sort of artificial stimulant — pizza. "The grease in the pizza lubricates the neurons and synapses in the brain," he says.

Poet A.E. Housman said he got himself started with a glass of beer and a brisk walk. He reported that the combination provoked the following happy effect: "As I went along, thinking nothing in particular . . . there would flow into my mind with sudden and unaccountable emotion, sometimes a line or two of verse, sometimes a whole stanza at once."

Many found their inspiration while walking. Wolfgang Amadeus Mozart, for example, said he could hear his compositions, all at once, "in a pleasing, lively dream," while he walked.

Robert Penn Warren says he "half-dreams" his poems while swimming. Humorist Dave Barry says he goes out and shoots baskets if he hits a writing block.

Other writers have used a variety of "tools" and rituals to help them create.

The poet Schiller kept rotten apples under the lid of his desk and inhaled the aroma while searching for the right word.

Victor Hugo wrote in the nude. Benjamin Franklin wrote while soaking in a bathtub.

Many wrote in bed, and Voltaire used his lover's naked back as a writing desk.

Hemingway wrote standing up (and told an interviewer, "The legs go first"). Thomas Wolfe, Virginia Woolf and Lewis Carroll also were standers.

Colette picked fleas from her cat while preparing to write.

Hart Crane wrote in the midst of loud parties. Bertolt Brecht liked to write in pubs. Contemporary writer Natalie Goldberg writes in cafés, with all the noise and confusion swirling around her. Mort Walker (creator of the "Beetle Bailey" and "Hi and Lois" cartoons) likes to come up with ideas by joking around with friends at parties. When he's alone and trying to create funny situations, he creates a party in his head.

Walker says he never waits for inspiration. Instead, he writes himself into a corner, just starts writing something, anything, sometimes churning out thirty ideas in an hour. Of those, perhaps five will be usable, but he says it beats taking a half an hour to try to scratch out one perfect idea.

No writing parties for Sinclair Lewis. He tried to remove all external distractions when he wrote. "Work in a bare room," he advised, "with nothing in it but a table, a chair and a typewriter, and enough light—but no view!"

Writer and teacher Brenda Ueland also found inspiration in quiet and solitude. She wrote that inspiration comes slowly and quietly and all the time and advised writers to be quiet, to think, to let ideas in. She felt that creative power could be frightened away by nervous straining.

Many write to music — for inspiration, for concentration and for rhythm.

Stendhal read two or three pages of the French Civil Code every morning before beginning work. Willa Cather read the Bible.

J.R.R. Tolkien prayed for inspiration and believed that his creativity was a gift from God.

Getting Started Is Often a Matter of Discipline

Sir Walter Scott, surely one of the most prolific writers (twenty-seven massive novels, a nine-volume biography of Napoleon, twelve volumes of collected letters, a journal that runs over seven hundred pages in print) always had two projects going, on two desktops. He rose at five and wrote until noon.

Charles Dickens, another prolific writer, also often had two or even three novels going at once. He almost always wrote at top speed, perhaps spurred by the fear of bankruptcy (his father had gone to debtors' prison).

Anthony Trollope provides an extreme example of scheduled, disciplined writing. He published sixty novels by writing for three hours each day, which, he wrote in his autobiography, "will produce as much as a man ought to write." He arose at 5:00 a.m., seven days a week, and was at his desk by 5:30 to reread the previous days' production. By 6:00 he would begin, clocking himself at 1,000-words per hour, 2,500-words per day. By 8:30 he was dressed for breakfast, and so off to a full day's work at the post office, where he was an official.

Whatever your approach, and however you structure your writing time, the most important step is to get something, anything, down on paper.

When you do, one word triggers another, one image explodes into a richer, more complex image, ideas begin forming chains, and you're on your way.

They'll be time to revise and edit later. In the beginning you must capture the energy and excitement and discover the unique perspective that will make your writing vivid and memorable.

■ ■ ■ ■ ■ ■ ■ ■ ■ ■ ■ ■ ■ ■
What's Got You Stuck?

Writer's block is a lot like a head cold. You feel all stuffed up. Nobody seems to be able to help you. And you'll probably get well pretty soon by yourself.

Like "flu" and "virus," "writer's block" is a generic term covering a variety of ailments. To know how to get yourself unstuck, you need to understand exactly what's sticking. Here are a few of the more common strains of writer's block, along with prescriptions for relief.

Writer's Blank: The Black Hole Syndrome. You keep finding gaping holes in your writing. Your writing gets fancier and fancier as you try to embroider around the edges.

℞: Go back three spaces to the research stage. Ask the right questions to the right people so you can fill in those blanks. Then you'll be ready and eager to write.

All Dressed Up and Nowhere to Go. You've done your re-search, you've made some time for writing, you're in your writing place—and you don't know where to begin.

℞: Go back two steps to the simmer stage. Reread your notes, looking for unifying themes and interesting abnormalities. Ask, "What would my reader want to know about this material?" Ask, "What's different about this material?"

So Many Leads, So Little Time. You're again at the keyboard, and this time you know exactly what you want to say. You just don't know how or where to begin. You feel overwhelmed by the subject.

℞: If it's a big project, break it down into small bits. In other words, don't sit down to write a novel. Sit down to write a scene. Then don't try to find the Right Way. Play "how many ways?" Discover as many possible beginnings as you can. Then pick a good one and get on with it.

In Other Words, There Are No Words. You know what you want to say and in what order. You know where to start and where you're likely to end up. But the words just won't come. Each syllable is a struggle. Each sentence seems worse than the last.

℞: Visualize. stop trying to make words and make pictures. Then keep plugging away, realizing that you'll have to revise anyway. Your reader will never know how you felt when you were writing.

Bathroom Bowl Sure Needs Cleaning. You'd rather do anything, *anything*, but write.

℞: Aversion often arises from fear. Figure out what you're afraid of. Are you ill-prepared? Have you skipped a step? Go back and do what needs to be done to get ready to write. Then make yourself a deal. Say you'll write for fifteen minutes. If your little mind and its surly mood get absorbed in the writing, you'll write yourself right out of the mood and into your subject. If not, at least you've accomplished fifteen minute's worth of writing. If you still feel like scrubbing the toilet bowl instead of writing, go for the Lysol.

The Space Cadet Syndrome. Your backside is in the chair, your fingers are on the keys, but your mind is in another galaxy.

℞: If the stuff you're writing can't keep you interested, how can you expect it to interest a reader? Ask yourself the following questions: What do I get for writing this? What does my reader get for reading it? Don't be afraid to rip out what you've written and start over, guided by a renewed sense of purpose and a re-commitment to never, never, never bore the reader.

Editor on My Shoulder. It just won't be good enough. It isn't right. It really stinks.

℞: First comes creation. Judgment day comes later. Knock the editor or critic off your shoulder and just let it rip.

Plato's Dilemma. The stuff on the page just isn't as good as the ideal form in your head. Something's getting lost in the translation.

℞: The stuff on the page *never* seems as good as the notion in the noggin. The airy conceptions of the mind can remain nebulous and incomplete. The moment you try to put them into words, you must give them specific shape and substance. What seemed limitless now has boundaries. Of course it's not as exciting. But it's more valuable. Keep writing.

Noddin' Noggin. Your brain feels like a flat tire looks. You don't have enough energy to think and press the keys at the same time. Your mind screams for sleep.

℞: You *could* take a nap. You might really be tired, after all. (A recent study suggests that 80 percent of Americans suffer from some degree of chronic sleep deprivation.) But it may just be that your system needs fresh air. Get up and move around. Then for next time, try to schedule your writing time to coincide with an energy peak instead of a trough.

Whatever brand of block you've got, there's a way through, around or over it. Recognize it for what it is and then get on with the writing.

13

Making the Trial Run

Some write slowly. They're unable to go on to the second sentence until they've buffed and polished the first. Others erupt first and clean up the mess later. Most of us fall somewhere in between the extremes.

I'm of the catharsis school of rough draft. Get it down on paper now; worry about what it says later. I've found it foolish to revise much as I go along, since I might cut much of the material later anyway. But obviously I try hard to say what I mean to say, and I do a lot of deleting and rearranging as I go.

Some are sprinters, working best in short, intense bursts. Others prefer the steady pace of the marathoner. Many learn to write for fifteen minutes or eight hours, depending on life circumstances. (I heard a football coach describe it this way: "You take whatever the defense gives you.")

There's no one right way to write. You must find your own way, your own creative pace.

But however you get the words onto paper, know this:

"Nobody Gets It Right the First Time"
Consider your first draft a trial run.

Even if you edit as you go, don't judge the overall worth of your project, the importance of your purpose, or your effectiveness in carrying out that purpose. You must withhold judgment, first because you're too close to the work to judge it effectively anyway, and second because to judge it now is to run the risk of turning off the creative tap and leaving yourself with nothing of value to judge later.

Lock the critics out. They have no place in the creative process.

Lock the editor out — but only for now. You'll need all of your critical skills later on. But first you need to capture the essence and the spirit.

Take chances. Play hunches. During the trial run, there's no such thing as a mistake, but only different possibilities, different ways to carry out your intention.

Say "yes" now. You can say "no" later if you need to.

Playing "How Many Ways?"

You know that the first few sentences and paragraphs are not only the toughest to write but also the most important. They determine whether or not editors buy and readers read. You're under a lot of pressure. You can stare, sweat, struggle, and otherwise work yourself into a state of two parts panic to one part stupor, trying to find the Right Way. Or you can eliminate all that wasted motion and play "How many ways?" instead.

I started using the "How many ways?" technique about five years ago. Now I wouldn't write without it. It's easy and fun, so I'm eager to get started. It carries me right past any potential writer's block.

Instead of trying to find the Right Way, I punch out as many ways to begin as I can think of. Sometimes I'll set myself a quota — a dozen potential leads, for example. Sometimes I'll give myself a time limit — how many leads can I generate in ten minutes? I try to discover as many approaches as possible. They may be serious or satirical, descriptive or expository. Each lead is a totally different approach, not simply a rewriting or fine-tuning of a previous approach.

As with all the other kinds of brainstorming we've talked about in this book, the key is a non-critical acceptance of each idea. Write them all down, without worrying about whether or not you'll be able to use them later. Don't even begin to think about how a reader might react to your ideas.

One idea leads to another. A "silly" idea triggers a wonderful one. A seeming dead end opens onto a new path.

Often the first three or four ideas I come up with are trite. I thought of them first because I've seen them often or recently or both. But I write them down anyway, freeing myself to get beyond them to fresher, more daring approaches.

Occasionally my first idea turns out to be the keeper. But the others still aren't wasted because they test the worth of that original approach and give me insight into how to write the rest of the piece.

I never discard the rejects. They often prove useful as transitions or internal leads within the body of the piece.

In fiction, I do the same sort of thing by starting my story at several different points in the action (usually the further into the action I start, the more exciting the opening scene). I'll also write the first scene from several points of view. This lets me discover the point of view that feels right and also helps me explore my characters' perceptions and motives.

No matter what you're writing, take a few minutes to explore possibilities before committing to a beginning.

Here are a few of the leads I created while playing "How many ways?" for an article on vitamins for *Madison Magazine*. (I went back later to add the commentary.)

> Vitamins are a three-billion-dollar-per-year-industry in America. Locally, Loyal "Sev" Severson, owner of the Madison Health Food Store on Monroe Street, has been selling vitamin and mineral supplements for over twenty years.

(Hit 'em with a big number, then follow up with the local angle.)

> College students are notorious for their eat-and-run approach to nutrition. Fast food and caffeine fuel many all-night study sessions, and students often lack time, opportunity and inclination to eat balanced meals.
>
> Pharmacist Jim Neuhauser, whose pharmacy is located just a few blocks from the University of Wisconsin-Madison campus, says he gets a lot of college students in asking about vitamins. "They're tired and run-down," Neuhauser says, "and they think if they take vitamins, they'll get all A's. But . . . they can't get all their meals at McDonalds."

(Student angle, plus local source quoted early. But students don't read this magazine.)

A well-balanced diet and moderate exercise—not mega-doses of vitamins—are still the best ways to promote good health, according to University of Wisconsin-Madison professor.
(Meat and potatoes. A trifle D-U-L-L.)

Vitamins may be killing many Americans!
This shocking conclusion comes from a University of Wisconsin-Madison professor, who warns that vitamins may be causing liver damage, anemia and even a "shock-like state" resembling a coma.
(Just right—for the *National Enquirer*.)

Fred Flintstone and Bugs Bunny want us to give our kids more vitamins.
Dr. Mel Weinswig says we may be overdoing it.
(Not bad. I should try it out on *Parents Magazine*. But this article isn't about kids.)

A University of Wisconsin-Madison professor is fighting a one-person crusade against the vitamin pill.
"The vitamin pushers are in it strictly for the money," according to Dr. Mel Weinswig . . .
(Zippy. Melodramatic. He said it, but it distorts his intention.)

The information on the side of a cereal box used to be pretty much limited to directions on how to send in for your Captain Midnight Secret Decoder Ring.
But that was back in nutritionally innocent times, when cereals could get away with calling themselves things like Sugar Pops and Sugar Jets, and Mom pushed bacon, eggs, whole milk, and other instruments of death on us as a "balanced diet."
No more . . .

This lead carried me right into the article. I just kept writing, and good old "How many ways?" had once again helped me to get started.

After you've explored the possibilities and come up with a tentative beginning, carry this sense of creative exploration over into the rest of the writing. Write to discover your themes and voices. Allow yourself to create surprises. Don't try to control the process too much. Get out of the way and let it happen.

Write fat. You can revise lean later.

Write as simply, as directly and as sincerely as possible, with little thought to style. Style should be an organic function of your material and will arise naturally if you let it.

You've thought of your reader a great deal as you formed your intention, melding subject and slant into idea. But as you create your trial run, write for the sake of the material and out of your sense of how that material must be presented. Don't let reader or editor or critic look over your shoulder. Escape from them, and from yourself, and into the work.

Word processing can help you create freely. By making it easier to delete, add and rearrange material, the computer eliminates the penalties for taking chances.

Taking Side Trips

If you've created an outline for your project (anything from a formal Roman numeral masterpiece to a scribbled note to yourself qualifies as an "outline"), you'll of course want to have it in front of you now. But you may find yourself departing from the outline as the writing leads you onto a new path. Let yourself be diverted. You may find the side road to be much better than the highway you had mapped out. You'll never know unless you travel at least part way down that side road. You can always back up and rejoin the main highway.

All of this writing fat and following side roads and taking chances is often messy and time-consuming. If you want to save time and avoid chaos, ignore these suggestions, stick to the outline and rein yourself in every time you feel a diversionary thought coming on. But if you want to discover the richness of invention and expression within you, give yourself every opportunity to let the good stuff come out.

Here are three more tips to help you get into the discovery mode as you begin your trial run.

1. Take a Closed-book Test

The night before your writing session, read over your notes and outlines. When you sit down to write the next day, set all those notes aside and write from memory.

You'll leave important points out, misspell names, get your facts and figures wrong. You'll have to correct all that later. But the closed-book test allows you to discover what's really most important and most memorable about your material.

And this technique enables you to escape the "cut and paste" system of writing, in which you simply fill in the blanks in your outline or notes. "Cut and paste" composition can result in flat, bloodless writing.

2. Play Twenty Questions

What would your reader want to know about the scene you're about to describe, the process you're about to explain, the person you're about to profile, the bit of action you're about to create? Brainstorming freely and uncritically, develop a list of questions you think your reader might like to ask, given the chance.

It's a fine way to explore your material, forcing you to focus on a specific point of view. It's also a sneaky way to coax yourself into creating an outline. You may be able to arrange the questions, from most to least important, and write your piece using the questions as a guide.

3. Begin Anywhere But the Beginning

"Begin at the beginning," writing teachers have advised for decades. But that refers to the organization of the finished product, not the process of writing it. The reader need never know where you started writing or in what order you wrote your material, as long as you get the pieces assembled properly later on.

Consider the way a director shoots the scenes that will later comprise a motion picture. One of the stars is only available for a few days, so all her scenes are shot in one clump and later edited into their proper places. Another actor is to be clean-shaven throughout the story but appears with a full beard for the final scene. He shoots the bearded scene first and then shaves for the "earlier" scenes.

Several scenes are to take place in the Badlands of South Dakota.

The director carts cast and crew to the location and shoots all the Badlands scenes at once, even though they will later be interspersed throughout the action.

I'm doing the same sort of thing with my baseball novel. I've got the first four chapters in what I now think will be the proper order. I've also written a scene in which a player finds out that his wife's father has died. I've written a full chapter—the most lively part of the book, I think—wherein the manager and the public address announcer get thrown out of a game. I've got a fragment of a chapter about a player's attempt to overcome his alcoholism. I've got another fragment in which the blind clubhouse man detects a flaw that's tipping the opposition off to which pitch one of the hurlers will throw.

I don't know where these bits will fit. I'm writing what I feel ready to write. Later I'll assemble the pieces and try to weave them together into a seamless narrative.

You don't have to write the first part first. Write what you're ready to write.

All these techniques work well. For me, though, nothing works better, more consistently, than "How many ways?"

Sustaining the Flow

If you know you won't be able to finish a project in one sitting, break the work into manageable chunks and set yourself a realistic goal for each writing session.

As I outlined this book, the material separated itself into fourteen major chunks, the 21-day miracle writing plan, and several "interludes," which I later integrated into other chapters. But I didn't write the book in sixteen or seventeen or twenty or twenty-five sittings. I set goals for each session by breaking chapters into subcategories.

Don't wait until you get stuck before quitting for the day. Try to end each session knowing how you want to start the next. Leave off in the middle of an idea, or even in the middle of a sentence.

If you quit when you're stuck, you'll carry around that stuck feeling in your subconscious, and it may grow into a real aversion to keeping your next writing appointment. We build writer's blocks out of such aversions.

If you know what comes next, you'll build up an anticipation and an eagerness to get back to your project, and you'll return to your labors fresh and ready to go.

When you write your last word for the day, sit still for a bit, pencil in hand or fingers on keyboard, to see if more wants to come. Let the creative fall-out settle. Often when you relax and mentally step back from your work, you'll receive insights you were too busy to entertain while you were writing.

I often end a writing session by reading over my day's output. This seems to contradict conventional wisdom about not editing or revising too soon after creation. But I've found that going over my work has two immediate benefits. First, I'm assured that those words I worked so hard to wrestle onto the page haven't gotten up and walked away. And second, in reviewing what I've written, I'm priming my subconscious to continue to sift and simmer, so that when I'm ready to revise my material, I may receive new gifts of insight along with creative ways to improve what I've written.

I don't do any heavy revision, but I often make notes and ask myself questions to guide me when I come back to the material later.

Now set your manuscript aside for a bit and then come back to it, as open to possibility and invention as you've been all the way through, for a session of creative revision.

14

Re-creation. Or, Is It Recreation?

I'm making the trial run on what will eventually turn into this chapter on a Friday morning in August. The sky outside my office window is turning that yellowish tint that promises a rouser of a thunderstorm, and soon. The writing is going well, has gone well, in fact, ever since I put down the first word of the first chapter—except for one real rough stretch. (Can you find it?) But even though the writing is going smoothly, I backtrack often, delete, insert, rearrange. I write a sentence in passive voice, reconsider, recast it in active voice.

Am I writing or revising? I must be writing, since I'm creating words that weren't there before. But I'm also doing things that look suspiciously like revision. The distinction between the two often isn't very clear. Although I've been told to banish the editor from the process of creation, it appears that I haven't been totally successful, haven't "transcended linear thought," as one of my students once claimed to have done after turning in a composition that contained not one punctuation mark or capital letter.

I've been told to lock you, my future reader, out of the creative process, too. As I create my trial run for this chapter, I try to let my thoughts flow freely and naturally. I try to phrase these thoughts with simplicity, clarity and sincerity. I write to please myself. But I'm fully aware that you will one day read these words. I'm aware of you, and so I must to some extent write for you, too.

When it comes time to revise and rewrite this chapter, the how-to books say I should try to banish my imp, with all its noisy, messy energy, and leave the job solely to my stern, orderly editor. But if I do so, will I edit the life and the fun right out of my writing? And will I miss new ideas, new inspirations, that could have enriched and informed my writing?

It's a false dilemma, created out of the left brain/right brain over-simplification and our need to try to give names to things we don't understand very well. There is no clear line between "writing" and "rewriting." You revise as you create; you re-create as you revise. You must bring all of yourself to each stage of the writing encounter. In your most creative moments, you still write with nouns and verbs, and you still want your words to make sense—not just any sense, but the precise sense you intend. And when you revise, you must remain open to discovering new insights and new excitement.

As we've walked through the creative process together, we've stressed the importance of withholding judgment. If you want to tap into your creative energies, releasing original and powerful ideas and images, you must get little mind out of the way, take chances, try out new combinations. Write first for the sake of the writing, we've said. Write to please yourself and your own sense of the rightness of what you're creating. To try to analyze too soon is to risk cutting off the creative flow and destroying the creative moment. Later for editing. Later for judging. Later for criticizing.

But it isn't your over-concern with subject/verb agreement that is most likely to hurt you in the early stages of creation. It's the temptation to close yourself to inspiration, to limit the flow of ideas, to ignore new possibilities, in order to write something "acceptable" and to get the job done as easily and painlessly as possible. You must risk inconvenience, risk pain, for the sake of the writing.

The editor and the reader are present in the act of creation, but you must not allow them to dominate. That's the great trick. Once you formulate your intention, which is all bound up in communicating something to a reader, you must try to set your awareness of that reader aside, lest you get too self-conscious and too careful. And you must quiet the grammarian/critic who would question every word, or else you risk not being able to write anything at all.

You're with me as I write this. You give me purpose and motivation. I smile as I imagine that you will like something I've written. My grammarian is here, too, and so the words come out pretty much in proper sentences and paragraphs. But my ideas and my passion dominate my consciousness. I become absorbed in the writing. You and the editor are only a faint presence, at the edge of awareness.

When it's time to revise, you will come forth and assume a much larger, more active role.

The Myth of Objectivity

You must revise your work "objectively," Those Who Know have told you.

I tried for years to be objective when I revised; I never once succeeded. I've never been able to read my own work dispassionately. That's another of those "left brain/right brain" myths. If you can reread your writing without feeling that thrill of recognition and that passionate caring that a parent feels for a child or a teacher for a student, you should quit writing. Your creation is a part of you. Your skill, your belief, whatever truth you have, are in your words. You can't not care about them.

You can edit *my* work objectively. As you've read this book, you've probably encountered dozens of passages you would have handled differently. But your work is your work. You care about it more than you care about my work. You can approach my work coldly. You can never approach your own work that way.

But you can approach it critically. You'd better be able to, if you want to write as well as you can. You can try to improve your creation, just as a parent tries—through example and instruction, reward and punishment—to shape a child's behavior and character.

In the revision stage, the emphasis shifts. You must now give every consideration to your future reader. Ask of yourself and of your writing:
- Have I been clear?
- Will the reader understand my references?
- Have I played fair with my reader, avoiding tricks and manipulation?
- Have I said what needs to be said, explained what needs to be explained—and not one word more?
- Have I respected my reader's intelligence?
- Have I remembered that the reader has other things to do besides read my stuff?

You'll need your inner editor's help here, because you must get all the words and punctuation marks flying in proper formation. Grammar is nothing more than a set of guidelines to help you tell the reader how to read your words. Writer and reader share a set of assumptions about what each word and each punctuation mark mean. If you want your reader to pause briefly, you insert a comma.

If you intend a full stop, you use a period (or, rarely, a semicolon). If you give me a wrong signal, you confuse me, perhaps frustrate me, maybe even lose my trust, which is the most important element binding me to you.

If you spell "night" N-I-T-E, you distract me from your thought and swing my attention, instead, to your grammar. I remember that I am reading and become aware again of the printed page, of the chair I'm sitting in and the way it hurts my back to sit in it too long, to the clock marking off time I might suddenly decide to spend in other ways. All that from "nite" or "comitment" or "wierd." It hardly seems fair.

If I've learned to like and trust you before I encounter the offending word, I may forgive you and read on. Or I may assume that you meant to do it. And then I'll wonder why and again become distracted from the point you had hoped to make or the emotion you had hoped to arouse and become conscious instead of myself as a reader and you as a writer.

If you litter the writing with enough "nites," I'll stop trusting you. If you can't spell correctly, if you can't get your commas in the right place, if you insist on dangling your modifiers in confusing and comic ways, I'll decide that you probably don't know what you're writing about.

Your inner editor helps you get the words spelled right and the modifiers lined up with their subjects. If she doesn't know the right spelling, she (I'm not really sure what gender your editor is, but "she" feels right today) sends you to the dictionary.

But such attention to grammar is an organic part of the creative process, not something you add later, like a garnish. You write with commas and periods just as surely as with words. You just have to be careful not to get too hung up on correctness during the trial run, because it can distract you from your mission and prevent you from becoming absorbed into your passion. Correct placement of commas and correct spelling of words are a part of writing, but writing is much more than correctness, and it's the "much more" that must concern you primarily in the creation stage. You'll edit carefully for precision later.

But again, it isn't a matter of grammar or no grammar. Just as passion and caring should pervade the process from the first flush of an idea to the finished work in print, so should a sense of using language carefully, respectfully and precisely.

Becoming Passionately Analytical

Trying to revise work that's still warm from the creative process is like trying to discipline a baby. In both cases, you're likely to be blind to the newborn's faults.

What could be more appealingly helpless than an infant? Sure, it cries and spits up and messes. But that's what it's supposed to do. You wouldn't think of punishing a baby for doing what is normal and necessary. And besides, if it's *your* crying, spitting mess-maker we're talking about, this child cries and spits and messes with more personality, more character and more native intelligence than any child who ever cried, spat and messed.

Later on, when your child is old enough to lock the dog in the broom closet and smear peanut butter on the bedsheets, you'll of course become involved in correction—often passionately so. You won't do so "objectively." You'll correct out of an intense love and an intense desire to amend behavior for the better.

So too with your writing. You won't want to discipline it right away, and you probably wouldn't be able to if you tried, but you'll certainly want and need to do so later.

As you write, you'll be caught up in the emotion of the moment. You may become elated or dejected or some of each. No matter what your state of mind, you aren't likely to do much productive revising.

These emotions have nothing to do with the quality of the work, remember. You're reacting to the process of creating. Whether you're hearing the siren song of ecstasy or the funeral dirge of despair, the emotions are not to be trusted. You should never act on them—sending your work off unedited, for example, or throwing it away unread.

Get some distance, not so that you can become "objective," but so that you become passionately analytical. How long is long enough? James Michener reputedly locked his manuscripts in a desk drawer for a year before revising them. Deadline writers make two quick phone calls, grab a cup of coffee and start attacking the story they finished only minutes before. Your ideal waiting period probably lies somewhere in between these extremes, and life will undoubtedly force you to come closer to the deadline writer than to Michener. But even a few minutes away from the work will help.

When you're ready to re-encounter your writing—whether after minutes or weeks — consider four different methods for improving that work and getting it ready for others to read: re-creating, revising, editing and proofreading.

1. Re-creating

You may be tempted to dive right in at page one and begin the sometimes exhilarating, often painful process of slashing and burning we call revision. But you might want to stay the knife for a bit and instead give yourself another opportunity to discover new insights, powerful images and felicitous phrases.

Instead of revising what you've written, first try writing it anew. Set the manuscript aside and write a second version, without referring to the original. This second version needn't be complete. You may want to re-create only a few sections.

Then set both versions aside, come back to them later and meld the best of both into a new creation.

2. Revising

When you begin the more traditional process of revising — reading your work carefully for organization and flow, trying to fill the gaps and eliminate the superfluous — don't shut off your creativity. By now your subconscious has had a long time to simmer. The imp may have new ideas and insights to share. Keep open to the possibilities. Listen to your intuitions.

The great temptation here, as in all steps in the writing process, is to hurry. The journey is almost over. You can smell the hay in the barn. You're weary. You can think of a hundred more pleasant tasks you'd rather be doing. If a new idea barges in now, it may ruin everything. A new lead forces a restructuring of the whole article. Reevaluation of the point of view character means you must recast the whole chapter. A slight shift in tone in one sentence sends ripples through the whole manuscript.

But your goal mustn't be simply to get the writing done. Your goal must be to make the writing as good as it can be, and to do so, you may need to write it new.

If the writing is good now, revise to make it better.

3. Editing

When it is better, edit to make it wonderful. Then edit one more time to bring it as close to perfection as you can.

Do your major cutting first, so that you won't spend a lot of time editing material only to slash it later.

I find it fairly easy and quite satisfying to cut out the garbage. "Every slaughtered syllable is a good deed done," the poet says. I feel almost gleeful as I slaughter these types of excess syllables:

• *Throat-clearing*. The "This topic is very important, and we should all pay strict attention to it" kind of blather we say just to soothe our nerves while we inch toward the point;

• *Baby Puppies*. The *past* history of the *entire* organization indicates that the *original* founder drew on a *general* consensus *of opinion* in formulating a *pre*plan . . .

• *Math Equations*. The "This was the place in which George Washington slept" formula. The problem with this sort of writing is that we tend to use empty constructions such as "The problem . . . is that" instead of simply saying "such writing uses empty constructions."

Hit the delete and watch the writing come into clearer focus.

Those are easy cuts. The tough cuts come when the writing is lean and clear—and maybe even clever—but not on the point. You must cut the marvelously witty, insightful paragraph that just doesn't have a lot to do with the topic at hand or that departs from the focus. If it makes you feel better, save the gem in a folder or on a disc. Just don't let it hurt the piece of writing you're working so hard to perfect.

Edit purposefully. Go through the work several times, if necessary, each time looking for specific ways to improve the writing. You know your weaknesses as a writer better than anyone else. If passive voice is a problem, take a pass through the work, looking for passive voice. Then create graceful ways to avoid it. If you tend to mix verb tenses, go on a verb-tense patrol.

To make sure you're making sense, create mental pictures of what you've written. Take your words literally. If you really see what you've written, you won't let a "Throw mama from the train a kiss" kind of confusion get by you, because you'll see the poor woman flying over the railing and onto the tracks.

Go beyond "good" and achieve "wonderful." Find the better

word. Transcend correctness. Dare to boldly break a rule (such as splitting an infinitive) if you feel that the "incorrect" construction conveys the thought/image/emotion more powerfully.

Reread your work aloud. Your ear will detect the rhythm and flow of the language, just as your reader, hearing your words in her head, will be sensitive to the way your language moves and feels. Your ear will catch the 187-word sentence that looked fine on paper. Your ear will hear how far wrong "the latest in convenience" can go between the page and the reader's mind.

4. Proofreading
When the work is as good as you can make it, go through it one more time, not gulping the words down in hurried phrases but stopping at each word, to make sure it's the right word, that it means what you intend it to mean, and that it's spelled correctly. Some folks have such a hard time proofreading, they do it backwards, just so they'll make sure to really look at each word.

It's a lot of work. But you must commit yourself to doing whatever's necessary to make the writing as good as it can be. There are no shortcuts on the writer's path. If you want an easy vocation, take up sword-swallowing.

And remember the dictum we developed in the last chapter:

Nobody Gets It Right the First Time
Hemingway admitted to revising a section of a novel thirty-seven times, "to get the words right." Good writers take the time to recreate, revise, edit and proofread.

The Myth of the Hostile Reader

It's no longer enough that the work please you. It must now please a reader. It must convey the thought, image and emotion you put into it. The gap between your mind and the mind of your reader can be broad and deep.

The more you know your reader, the better able you'll be to bridge that gap. If you're writing a nonfiction article, you've probably had to study your target publication carefully in order to sell the idea to an editor. That means you've also studied your reader. Fiction is trickier, but you'll make adjustments in the way you approach your material depending upon whether you'll try to publish in a fine literary magazine like *Cutbank*, in a quality glossy such as *Redbook*, or in a "men's adventure" publication such as *Hustler*, for example.

Readers are a diverse lot, and every publication or press serves a different readership segment. But we can make some generalizations about readers, and perhaps exorcise one destructive misconception.

The Myth of the Hostile Reader stars a hypercritical, overbearing curmudgeon who reads primarily to find fault. She pounces on grammar errors, delights in inept, obvious plot twists, trembles with glee at every inconsistency. The only higher joy for this monster involves exposing the error — the more public the exposure, the better.

No wonder you get blocked if you try to write for such an ogre.

Don't write for her. She doesn't exist. If she did, you would be a fool to let her into your writing process — at any stage.

Sure, some folks are critical. And sure, they're quick to point out errors. I've gotten my share of critical letters, and I'm grateful for every one. (Well, *almost* every one.) If someone takes the time to help me become a better writer, I owe them thanks.

But most folks don't read in order to find mistakes. They read to learn and to be entertained. They read to share what you're offering. Your reader is basically good-hearted and wants you to succeed. "Dazzle me," she says as she scans the first few pages of your novel. "Teach me," she insists as she reads the lead of your how-to article. Show me new worlds. Move me.

Aren't you reading this book in order to learn and share and grow — and not to find out how many mistakes some guy named Cook might make? And haven't you given me the benefit of the doubt (or perhaps many doubts) by staying with me for so long? You would turn on me, and rightfully so, only if I betrayed your trust with sloppy writing, inaccurate reporting, dishonesty, insincerity or disrespect.

Portrait of the Good-hearted Grazer

I know you're good-hearted. But I also know that you're busy and that you're flooded with print. I know that because I'm one of you.

Let's analyze your typical encounter with the printed page. Let's suppose that you subscribe to a magazine called *Writer's Digest*. Let's further suppose that you invite this fine publication into your home each month. You pay perfectly good money for it. You curl up with it eagerly (or at least the editors hope you do). But you don't plan to read every word on every page (no editor would expect you to). And even though you've sought out this magazine, one of your prime motives once you pick it up is to get through it and get on to all of the other things demanding your time and attention.

You're not yet a reader. You're a grazer, foraging through the pages, looking for nourishment and excitement. Headlines, graphics and leads compete for your attention. Flabby, pointless writing makes you turn the page quickly. Turn enough pages without stopping and you'll decide not to invite this magazine into your home anymore.

When I edit my stuff for *Writer's Digest* — or for any other publication — I remember just how busy you are. I'd better offer you something of real worth — useful or interesting information, a good time, an opportunity to explore — in the first twenty-five words or so or you'll move on — not because you're hostile, but simply because you're busy and selective. The busier you get, the more selective you become.

Just as I must respect the complexity of your life, I must also respect your intelligence. You're as smart as I am. I must believe that I have something to offer you — perhaps some information you haven't run across elsewhere; something I've learned in twenty-five years of writing and teaching; a different way of looking at things — or else I've no business writing for you. But I offer my insights, such as they are, to an intellectual equal. Talking down to you would not only be pompous and insulting. It would be wrong.

When I revise, then, it's for you, a good-natured, busy and intelligent reader.

Bringing Others Into the Act

Even though you've put some distance between creation and revision, and even though you've tried to see your work through your reader's eyes when you revise and edit, you still might be too close to it to do an effective job. A second set of eyes, attached to a different way of looking at the world, can bring a useful perspective to your manuscript.

But don't show your work to others until you and it are ready. Never show someone a rough draft. You'll waste their time, and you may subject them to an unpleasant reading experience. And besides, you probably already know what they'd be able to tell you about the work (namely that it's a rough draft with lots of problems needing your attention). Ask someone to be your reader; don't ask her to be your garbage collector. Show finished or nearly finished work.

Be ready to hear negative as well as positive comments. If you only want praise, send the work to a subsidy publisher. They'll tell you you're the finest writer who ever lived.

Don't give your work to someone if honest criticism from that person will hurt your relationship.

I'd also advise against showing your work to the sources you used in creating it. Check facts and quotes, yes — over the phone. But the way you shape and craft your material into a finished piece is your responsibility, not your subject's. If you show the piece to them before it has been published, they'll offer suggestions — often quite forcefully — for revision. (The percentage of folks who will totally like your profile of them is roughly equal to the percentage of folks who like their driver's license photos.) What then? Do you make changes and risk hurting the piece? Or do you leave it alone and risk hurting your relationship with the subject?

"If you weren't going to change it," the subject may ask, "why did you show it to me?" Good question.

Don't put your potential critic on the spot with a vague "How do you like it?" Ask specific questions in order to solicit the type of feedback you want and need. "Was the dialogue realistic?" Or even more specifically, "Could you tell the characters apart by the way they talk?"

Show your technical work to experts on your subject. They'll tell you whether or not you've got your facts straight. But show it to non-experts, too. They'll let you know whether or not your stuff makes sense.

Remind yourself that the criticism is directed at your work, not at you. Although you are in the writing, the writing is not you. It's a product of your skill and your will, and it's a projection of self, certainly, but separate, nevertheless.

Remember, too, that the reader is reacting out of a subjective interpretation of what you've written. Each reader will have a different response. Each response should be important to you, but no one response should be devastating.

Separate serious criticism from thoughtless put-down. "Your dialogue seemed stiff" is serious criticism. So is "I couldn't understand what you were getting at in your lead" or "the fourth paragraph doesn't make any sense." But "Maybe you should take up basket weaving" doesn't deserve much attention.

Others can teach you a great deal—not because they're experts, not because they're trained critics, and not because they're great writers—but because they can offer you fresh insight, a different viewpoint, an honest reaction. If several people tell you the same thing, listen hard. You're hearing the voice of your reader.

But criticism has its limits. Don't let negative comments wound too deeply, and don't let praise puff you.

Nobody can tell you what you ought to write or how to be faithful to your own vision. Let criticism inform our evaluation of your work. Reread your material in light of the insights others offer. Then make your own decisions. It's your writing; it must reflect your insight and vision.

If it doesn't, there's no point in writing it.

Valedictory: The 21-Day Miracle Writing Plan

You've researched. You've simmered and stewed and creatively procrastinated. You've outlined, using one of our free-flow methods, or a combination of methods, or no method at all.

You're ready to start writing. But before you do, I want to suggest a method to enable you to bring your most open and creative self to every writing encounter. Are you willing to invest thirty minutes a day for the next twenty-one days in a project that will help you tap into that surging river of original ideas and images that flows constantly through your subconscious? This simple project will enhance your writing fluency and strengthen the tie between your good ideas and the words you labor to create on the page.

And you absolutely can't fail. If you put in your thirty minutes a day for three full weeks, following a few simple rules, you will increase the quantity and quality of creative ideas in your writing.

Are you willing to try?

And are you willing to accept the consequences when you succeed? Are you willing to have your negative assumptions about yourself as a writer annihilated? Are you willing to blast through your limitations? Are you willing to be kept awake nights by the excitement of new ideas that won't wait until morning?

If you are, buy yourself a thick, spiral notebook and the kind of pen or pencil you're most comfortable with. Don't use old stuff. This project deserves new.

Find a writing place.

Make thirty minutes a day.

Use that thirty minutes to write.

Write about your problems. Write about your life. Make up a story. Write a letter to Jesus or Gandhi or Robert E. Lee or Babe

Ruth or whomever you'd like. Answer your own letter. Describe the first person you ever kissed and meant it. Describe what you look like to your dog or cat. Write a journal entry while pretending to be somebody else.

Write whatever you want, but follow these three guidelines.

■ ■ ■ ■ ■ ■ ■ ■ ■ ■ ■

1. Don't Stop
Keep writing, no matter what. Don't let your pen or pencil stop for the full thirty minutes.

2. Don't Think
Don't analyze, evaluate, criticize or calculate. Your creator loves you and wants to help you soar. Your critic isn't so sure about you or your writing and will trip you and wrestle you to the ground if you let it.

3. Don't Lie
Don't write what you think you ought to write. Write what you really want to write. Don't write what you've learned to be true. Write what you believe.

If possible, try doing this exercise first thing in the morning. You may find that you're more in touch with the muse when you're still half-dreaming.

Follow this regimen for thirty minutes a day for twenty-one days. You'll lose your self-consciousness and start a flow you couldn't dam up again if you tried. Free, honest writing will become a habit.

Don't think about doing it. Don't tell yourself you should do it. Just do it. Start today.

On the twenty-second day, go back and read what you've written. You'll be amazed by how original and creative your writing is.

Then keep right on writing.

Epilogue

The Writer's Last Hurrah

Just now, as I sat down to write to you for the final time (I'm actually writing the prologue last, amazingly enough), I had one final insight about the relationship between writer and reader.

I realized how much I'll miss you.

Writing this book has been like having an infinitely patient friend to talk to each day, about a subject I care for passionately. As I thought about that, I started to think about missing "it," this book, into which I've poured so much of myself over the last year. But it's not an "it" I'll miss. It's a "you," the you I've been imagining as I wrote for all these months.

I've learned so much from writing this book. I thank you for that. I've learned about the subject matter and how I feel about it. And I've learned about myself. My observations, my "rules," my "truths" kept changing on me as I wrote. It's that kind of subject. We'll never get done exploring it. It's tough to shoot a moving target, so consider this more of a movie than a still life.

I suspect I'll have to write another book to keep the conversation going. When I do, I'll probably contradict some of the things I've said here. If you read both and get confused, forgive me. Creativity is like that. We can pretty well track how the brain works now, but we've never really figured out where the mind is. The whole is just so much greater than the sum of its parts.

I don't want to end this conversation without giving you another list of three, my last bit of advice, at least for now.

1. You Can Do This Stuff

Decide what you want to do, figure out how to do it, and then devote yourself to doing it. Do whatever it takes to get it done.

You'll teach yourself whatever you need to know. If big mind doesn't already know it, you will intuitively know where to find the answers and how to seek them out.

Write from your truth. Trust yourself. Don't try to control. Let the writing happen through you. When you get down to your truth, it will be good. You don't need to be afraid of it.

2. You Don't Have to Do This Stuff

I hope you haven't waited until you finish this book to start or restart your life as a writer. I hope you've been making journal entries, staring at trees, flow-writing and in many other ways being a writer.

But if you haven't, if reading my words has, instead of energizing you, created a leaden feeling of dread in your guts, if you feel that I am ordering you to do something you really don't want to do — then don't. Being a writer is a want-to, not a have-to. There are hundreds of other ways to express your innate creativity. Keep exploring. You'll find yours.

3. It Ain't Necessarily Easy

If you've been writing for anytime at all, you know the truth of this last observation. I think writing is wonderful. I wouldn't want to think of living my life without it. But sometimes it's so hard, I feel I'll break under its demands. Sometimes it won't leave me alone, when I so want to be left alone. Sometimes I don't think I'll ever know enough or ever be brave enough, honest enough, to do justice to it.

But I guess no true calling is ever supposed to be easy.

I said three final observations, but I can't bear to leave you without making one more:

4. It Ain't Necessarily So, Just Because I Said It's So

A wonderful writer/teacher named Rivers taught me the rule every reporter must know: Verify everything. If your mother says she loves you, get a second source.

That's true for everything I've said in this book. Don't believe it, just because I said it and Writer's Digest Books published it and your bookstore sold it to you. Verify everything. In this case, your second source is your own intuition and your own experience. See if my observations stand up against yours. Try out techniques and see how they work for you. Adopt, alter, abandon as you see fit.

As we've noted so often during our journey together, you've got to do this your way.

May your journey fill you with wonder.

I hope you'll let me hear from you along the way, so that our conversation can continue.

Index

Other Books of Interest

General Writing Books
A Beginner's Guide to Getting Published, Editors of *Writer's Digest* magazine $16.95
Beginning Writer's Answer Book, Editors of *Writer's Digest* magazine $16.95
Dare to Be a Great Writer, by Leonard Bishop (paper) $14.95
Discovering the Writer Within, by Bruce Ballenger & Barry Lane $18.95
Essential Software for Writers: A Complete Guide for Everyone Who Writes with a PC, by Hy Bender (paper) $24.95
Getting the Words Right: How to Rewrite, Edit and Revise, by Theodore A. Rees Cheney (paper) $12.95
How to Write a Book Proposal, by Michael Larsen (paper) $11.95
How to Write Fast While Writing Well, by David Fryxell $17.95
How to Write with the Skill of a Master and the Genius of a Child, by Marshall J. Cook $7.58
Just Open a Vein, edited by William Brohaugh $6.99
Knowing Where to Look: The Ultimate Guide to Research, by Lois Horowitz (paper) $19.95
Make Your Words Work, by Gary Provost (paper) $14.95
On Being a Writer, edited by Bill Strickland (paper) $16.95
Pinckert's Practical Grammar, by Robert C. Pinckert (paper) $3.99
Research & Writing: A Complete Guide and Handbook, by Shah Malmoud (paper) $18.95
Shift Your Writing Career into High Gear, by Gene Perret $16.95
Thesaurus of Alternatives to Worn-Out Words and Phrases, by Robert Hartwell Fiske $17.99
The 30-Minute Writer: How to Write and Sell Short Pieces, by Connie Emerson $17.95
30 Steps to Becoming a Writer, by Scott Edelstein $16.95
The 28 Biggest Writing Blunders, by William Noble $12.95
The 29 Most Common Writing Mistakes & How to Avoid Them, by Judy Delton (paper) $9.95
The Wordwatcher's Guide to Good Writing & Grammar, by Morton S. Freeman (paper) $15.95
The Writer's Book of Checklists, by Scott Edelstein $16.95
The Writer's Digest Guide to Good Writing, Editors of *Writer's Digest* magazine $18.95
The Writer's Digest Guide to Manuscript Formats, by Buchman & Groves $18.95
The Writer's Essential Desk Reference, edited by Glenda Neff $19.95
Write Tight: How to Keep Your Prose Sharp, Focused and Concise, by William Brohaugh $16.95
Writing as a Road to Self-Discovery, by Barry Lane $16.95
Nonfiction Writing
The Complete Guide to Writing Biographies, by Ted Schwarz $6.99
How to Do Leaflets, Newsletters, & Newspapers, by Nancy Brigham (paper) $14.95
How to Write Irresistible Query Letters, by Lisa Collier Cool (paper) $10.95
The Complete Guide to Magazine Article Writing, by John M. Wilson $17.95
Magazine Writing That Sells, by Don McKinney $16.95
The Writer's Complete Guide to Conducting Interviews, by Michael Schumacher $14.95
The Writer's Digest Handbook of Magazine Article Writing, edited by Jean M. Fredette (paper) $12.95

Writing Articles From the Heart: How to Write & Sell Your Life Experiences, by Marjorie Holmes $16.95

Fiction Writing

Beginnings, Middles and Ends, by Nancy Kress $13.95
Best Stories from New Writers, edited by Linda Sanders $5.99
Characters & Viewpoint, by Orson Scott Card $14.95
The Complete Guide to Writing Fiction, by Barnaby Conrad $18.95
Conflict, Action & Suspense, William Noble $14.95
Creating Characters: How to Build Story People, by Dwight V. Swain (paper) $14.99
Dialogue, by Lewis Turco $13.95
The Fiction Writer's Silent Partner, by Martin Roth $19.95
Get That Novel Started! (And Keep Going 'Til You Finish), by Donna Levin $17.95
Handbook of Short Story Writing: Vol. I, by Dickson and Smythe (paper) $12.95
Handbook of Short Story Writing: Vol. II, edited by Jean Fredette (paper) $12.95
How to Write & Sell Your First Novel, by Collier & Leighton (paper) $13.95
Manuscript Submission, by Scott Edelstein $14.99
Mastering Fiction Writing, by Kit Reed $6.99
Plot, by Ansen Dibell $14.95
Practical Tips for Writing Popular Fiction, by Robyn Carr $17.95
Scene and Structure by Jack Bickham $14.95
Setting, Jack M. Bickham $14.95
Theme & Strategy, by Ronald B. Tobias $14.95
The 38 Most Common Fiction Writing Mistakes, by Jack M. Bickham $12.95
20 Master Plots (And How to Build Them), by Ronald B. Tobias $16.95
The Writer's Digest Character Naming Sourcebook, Sherrilyn Kenyon with Hal Blythe & Charlie Sweet $18.95
Writer's Digest Handbook of Novel Writing, $18.95
Writing the Blockbuster Novel, Albert Zuckerman, with Introduction by Ken Follett $17.95
Writing the Novel: From Plot to Print, by Lawrence Block (paper) $11.95
Writing the Short Story: A Hands-On Program, by Jack M. Bickham $16.99

Special Interest Writing Books

Armed & Dangerous: A Writer's Guide to Weapons, by Michael Newton (paper) $15.95
The Art and Craft of Poetry, Michael J. Bugeja $19.95
Cause of Death: A Writer's Guide to Death, Murder & Forensic Medicine, by Keith D. Wilson, M.D. $15.95
Children's Writer's Word Book, by Alijandra Mogliner $19.95
Comedy Writing Secrets, by Mel Helitzer (paper) $15.95
The Complete Book of Feature Writing, by Leonard Witt $18.95
The Craft of Writing Science Fiction That Sells, Ben Bova $16.95
Creating Poetry, by John Drury $18.95
Deadly Doses: A Writer's Guide to Poisons, by Serita Deborah Stevens with Anne Klarner (paper) $16.95
Editing Your Newsletter, by Mark Beach (paper) $18.95
Families Writing, by Peter Stillman (paper) $12.95
A Guide to Travel Writing & Photography, by Ann & Carl Purcell (paper) $22.95
How to Pitch & Sell Your TV Script, by David Silver $6.99
How to Write and Sell Children's Picture Books, by Jean E. Karl $16.95
How to Write & Sell Greeting Cards, Bumper Stickers, T-Shirts and Other Fun Stuff, by Molly Wigand (paper) 15.95
How to Write & Sell True Crime, by Gary Provost $5.99
How to Write Horror Fiction, by William F. Nolan $15.95
How to Write Mysteries, by Shannon OCork $14.95
How to Write Romances, by Phyllis Taylor Pianka $15.95
How to Write Science Fiction & Fantasy, by Orson Scott Card $13.95
How to Write Tales of Horror, Fantasy & Science Fiction, edited by J.N. Williamson (paper) $12.95
How to Write the Story of Your Life, by Frank P. Thomas (paper) $12.95
How to Write Western Novels, by Matt Braun $1.00
The Poet's Handbook, by Judson Jerome (paper) $12.95
Police Procedural: A Writer's Guide to the Police and How They Work, by Russell Bintliff (paper) $16.95
Powerful Business Writing, by Tom McKeown $3.95
Private Eyes: A Writer's Guide to Private Investigators, by H. Blythe, C. Sweet, & J. Landreth (paper) $15.95
Scene of the Crime: A Writer's Guide to Crime-Scene Investigation, by Anne Wingate, Ph.D. $15.95

Successful Scriptwriting, by Jurgen Wolff & Kerry Cox (paper) $14.95
The Writer's Complete Crime Reference, by Martin Roth $19.95
The Writer's Guide to Conquering the Magazine Market, by Connie Emerson $17.95
The Writer's Guide to Creating a Science Fiction Universe, by George Ochoa & Jeff Osier $18.95
The Writer's Guide to Everyday Life in the 1800s, by Marc McCutcheon $18.95
Writing for Children & Teenagers, 3rd Edition, by L. Wyndham & Arnold Madison (paper) $12.95
Writing Mysteries: A Handbook by the Mystery Writers of America, Edited by Sue Grafton, $18.95
Writing the Modern Mystery, by Barbara Norville (paper) $12.95

The Writing Business
Business & Legal Forms for Authors & Self-Publishers, by Tad Crawford (paper) $4.99
The Complete Guide to Self-Publishing, by Tom & Marilyn Ross $18.99
This Business of Writing, by Gregg Levoy $7.98

To order directly from the publisher, include $3.00 postage and handling for 1 book and $1.00 for each additional book. Allow 30 days for delivery.
(paper) $15.95
Scene of the Crime: A Writer's Guide to Crime-Scene Investigation, by Anne Wingate, Ph.D. $15.95
Successful Scriptwriting, by Jurgen Wolff & Kerry Cox (paper) $14.95
The Writer's Complete Crime Reference, by Martin Roth $19.95
The Writer's Guide to Conquering the Magazine Market, by Connie Emerson $17.95
The Writer's Guide to Creating a Science Fiction Universe, by George Ochoa & Jeff Osier $18.95
The Writer's Guide to Everyday Life in the 1800s, by Marc McCutcheon $18.95
Writing for Children & Teenagers, 3rd Edition, by L. Wyndham & Arnold Madison (paper) $12.95
Writing Mysteries: A Handbook by the Mystery Writers of America, Edited by Sue Grafton, $18.95
Writing the Modern Mystery, by Barbara Norville (paper) $12.95

The Writing Business
Business & Legal Forms for Authors & Self-Publishers, by Tad Crawford (paper) $4.99
The Complete Guide to Self-Publishing, by Tom & Marilyn Ross $18.99
This Business of Writing, by Gregg Levoy $7.98

To order directly from the publisher, include $3.00 postage and handling for 1 book and $1.00 for each additional book. Allow 30 days for delivery.